In the Field

Recent view of the Kelsey Museum of Archaeology. Photo: Bill Wood.

In the Field

The Archaeological Expeditions of the Kelsey Museum

Lauren E. Talalay
and Susan E. Alcock

Kelsey Museum Publication 4
Ann Arbor, Michigan, 2006

Published by
Kelsey Museum of Archaeology
The University of Michigan
434 South State Street
Ann Arbor, MI 48109-1390
USA

Manufactured in China

ISBN 0-9741873-3-X

Front cover image: A general view of excavations in progress at Karanis, with Expedition Director Enoch E. Peterson at left, ca. 1927. Photo: G. R. Swain. 5.2927.

Back cover image: A member of the Pylos Regional Archaeological Project explores the remains of the subterranean heating system of a Roman bath, ca. 1994. Photo: S. E. Alcock.

This book is available direct from
The David Brown Book Company
PO Box 511, Oakville, CT 06779, USA
(Telephone 860-945-9329; Fax 860-945-9468)

and

Park End Place, Oxford OX1 1HN
United Kingdom
(Telephone 01865-241249; Fax 01865-794449)
www.oxbowbooks.com

Contents

ACKNOWLEDGMENTS 6

INTRODUCTION 8

MAP: LOCATIONS OF KELSEY MUSEUM FIELDWORK 11

EXCAVATIONS AND REGIONAL SURVEYS
Antioch of Pisidia, Turkey, 1924 12
Karanis, Egypt, 1924–1935 16
Carthage, Tunisia, 1925, 1975–1979, 1982–1987 20
Seleucia-on-the-Tigris, Iraq, 1927–1932, 1936–1937 26
Sepphoris, Israel, 1931 30
Soknopaiou Nesos (Dimé), Egypt, 1931–1932 32
Terenouthis, Egypt, 1935 34
Monastery of St. Catherine at Mount Sinai, Egypt, 1958, 1960, 1963, 1965 36
Qasr al-Hayr al-Sharqi, Syria, 1964, 1966, 1969–1971 40
Apollonia, Libya, 1965–1967; Cyrene, Libya, 1969, 1971, 1973–1981 44
Tel Anafa, Israel, 1968–1973, 1978–1986 48
Dibsi Faraj, Syria, 1972–1974 52
Paestum-Poseidonia, Italy, 1981–1986, 1995–1998 54
Coptos and the Eastern Desert, Egypt, 1987–1995 58
Leptiminus Archaeological Project, Tunisia, 1990–1999 64
Pylos Regional Archaeological Project, Greece, 1991–1996 70
Southern Euboea Exploration Project, Greece, 1996, 2000, 2002, 2005 74
The Abydos Middle Cemetery Project, Egypt, 1995– 78
Kedesh of the Upper Galilee, Israel, 1997– 84
The Vorotan Project, Armenia, 2005– 88

BIBLIOGRAPHY 90

PHOTO CREDITS 103

Acknowledgments

A roster of dedicated individuals has helped bring Kelsey-sponsored projects to fruition, and many foundations and granting agencies have supported the Museum's efforts. Although the sponsors are not listed in the individual entries that follow, we would like to acknowledge the invaluable support over the years of several major institutions: the American Research Center in Egypt, the Fulbright Program; the Corning Museum of Glass; the Institute for Aegean Prehistory; the National Endowment for the Humanities; the National Geographic Society; the Smithsonian Institution; the Social Sciences and Humanities Research Council of Canada; and the United States Information Agency. Several universities have also provided funding, namely, the Universities of Cincinnati, Minnesota, Missouri, and Pennsylvania, together with Dumbarton Oaks, in the United States and the Universities of Manitoba and Toronto in Canada, as well as the University of Cambridge in Great Britain, the University of Perugia in Italy, and Assiut University in Egypt. The University of Michigan has offered a deep well of funding over the decades, in which we have repeatedly dipped our bucket; we would particularly like to acknowledge the very generous support of the Office of the Vice President for Research and the Horace H. Rackham School of Graduate Studies.

In addition, a number of vital national institutions have welcomed Kelsey projects over the years and granted permission for their work; we thank particularly the Greek Ministry of Culture's Central Archaeological Council (KAS); the Institute of Archaeology and Ethnography, National Academy of Sciences, Armenia; the Institut National du Patrimoine, Tunisia; the Israel Antiquities Authority; the Libyan Antiquities Service; the Soprintendenza Antichità e Belle Arti of Salerno, Benevento, and Avellino; the Supreme Council of Antiquities (Ministry of Culture), Egypt; and the Syrian Department of Antiquities. Other institutions similarly extended warm hospitality and assistance to all involved in Kelsey fieldwork; we are grateful to the American Research Center in Egypt, the American School of Classical Studies in Athens, and various US foreign services and embassies throughout the Mediterranean. Entries for this book were provided by John F. Cherry (Vorotan Project), Sharon Herbert (Tel Anafa, Coptos and the Eastern Desert, and Kedesh of the Uppper Galilee), Janet Richards (The Abydos Middle Cemetery Project), and David Stone (Leptiminus); all other descriptions are the work of the authors, with much help from various project participants. Funding for this volume was provided by the John H. D'Arms Collegiate Professorship in Classical Archaeology and Classics and by a generous gift to the Kelsey Museum of Archaeology from James J. and Ann Duderstadt.

Finally, we would like to offer our sincerest appreciation to all of the individuals who provided information, text, and images on the various projects described below: Geoffrey Compton, Ilene Forsyth, Sharon Herbert, James Higginbotham, Donald Keller, Robin Meador-Woodruff, John Pedley, Janet Richards, Lea Stirling, David Stone, and Andrew Wilburn. We also acknowledge the generosity of Professor Ilene Forsyth and the Michigan-Princeton-Alexandria Expeditions to Mount Sinai; all photographs of the Monastery of St. Catherine at Mount Sinai are reproduced through the courtesy of that archive. Similarly, the illustrations for Dibsi Faraj are reproduced with the permission of Dumbarton Oaks, Trustees for Harvard University, and a photograph of Francis Kelsey appears through the courtesy of the Bentley Historical Library, University of Michigan. For assistance in gathering and scanning images, we thank Benjamin Eisman, Jennifer Gates, Andrew Wilburn, and especially Kate Carras. The map of project locations was created and designed by Lorene Sterner, to whom we are most grateful. Finally, we owe special thanks to John Cherry for his general assistance and editing, to Lori Khatchadourian and Sebastián Encina for help with proofreading, to Julia Falkovitch-Khain for endless hours spent in the library tracking down bibliographic references, and, as always, to the Kelsey Museum's exceptional editor and designer, Margaret Lourie, for her unfailing eye and infinite patience.

The images collected in this volume range in date from the early twentieth century to the present day. They represent the development of photographic technologies from large view cameras and tripods (with glass plate negatives) to high-resolution digital imagery. Many of the pictures reproduced are drawn from various photo archives of the Kelsey Museum of Archaeology; these are identified, in the caption, by their archival number. Otherwise the individual who kindly provided images is noted either in entry headings or in captions. A complete list of "Photo Credits" is provided on page 103.

Introduction

Photograph of Francis W. Kelsey taken in the 1920s. 5.7963.

By all accounts, Frances W. Kelsey was an extraordinary individual. Professor of Latin Language and Literature at the University of Michigan from 1889 until his death in 1927, Kelsey was an enthusiastic teacher, meticulous researcher, and savvy entrepreneur, who continually immersed himself in visionary projects, ranging from the archaeological to the humanitarian. There were, however, two particular missions that consumed much of his energy: the collection of antiquities from the Mediterranean and Near East, and the mounting of ongoing excavations in these same areas. Although he began acquiring archaeological objects and works of art in the late 1800s, his dreams of launching a series of excavations were not realized until 1924, in an archaeological era now associated with Indiana Jones—an archaeologist with very different objectives and methods than Francis Kelsey. With the aid of funds from a newly formed Near East Research Fund, Kelsey initiated two excavations that year, one in Turkey and the other in Egypt. Since that time, the University of Michigan and the Kelsey Museum of Archaeology have helped support nearly 20 more excavations and surveys in ten different countries throughout the Mediterranean and Near East.

The first Kelsey-supported "digs" focused on two distinctly different sites, Karanis, a Graeco-Roman town in northern Egypt, and Antioch of Pisidia, one of the most important Roman colonies in Asia Minor. The rural village of Karanis would prove to be the Kelsey Museum's signature site, yielding massive numbers of finds, 45,000 of which were shipped to Ann Arbor between 1926 and 1935. The Kelsey expedition's careful recording of finds at Karanis, labeled the "Pompeii of Egypt," opened a new window onto everyday life in Graeco-Roman Egypt. Today, the Kelsey's collection represents the finest assemblage of daily-life objects from that period to be found outside of the Cairo Museum.

Kelsey-sponsored fieldwork between the two world wars was not confined, however, to Karanis and Antioch. Work at other important sites in Egypt, North Africa, Israel, and Iraq was attracting the attention of scholars: Carthage, the famous city-state founded by the Phoenicians in the 9th century BC; Soknopaiou Nesos, a Graeco-Roman frontier town in northern Egypt; Terenouthis, a long-lived Egyptian necropolis with tombs ranging from the Middle Kingdom to the Roman period; Seleucia-on-the-Tigris, the eastern capital of the Selucid empire located at a well-traveled crossroads in present-day Iraq; and Sepphoris, a site in ancient Palestine that later would produce some of the finest mosaics of the Roman world.

Kelsey fieldwork was halted during World War II, however, and did not resume until the mid-1950s, when the Museum again sponsored a series of projects, this time mostly in Libya and Syria. Work was carried out at the Monastery of St. Catherine's, an isolated stronghold on Mount Sinai that maintained a small working monastic order; Qasr al-Hayr al-Sharqi, a medieval Islamic town located at the foot of one of the few mountain passes in the central Syrian desert; Cyrene, an affluent settlement in Libya occupied for more than 1,000 years during Greek, Hellenistic, and Roman times; Libyan Apollonia, the seaport of ancient Cyrene; and Dibsi Faraj, a late Roman and Byzantine "fortress city" in Syria.

Opposite page: Francis Kelsey (right) conversing with a local artist in Pompeii, 1892–1893. Kelsey 128.

Although the Museum's efforts from the 1980s to the early years of the 21st century still concentrated on circum-Mediterranean sites, significant shifts in orientation were clearly under way. In common with other academic disciplines, archaeology was undergoing a transformation, thanks both to increasing theoretical self-reflection and a growing openness to scientific and technological developments. While questions of chronology and description were still vital to the field, archaeologists began to focus on well-defined research objectives, more explicit and quantitative procedures, and a greater concern with regional, as opposed to site-based, approaches. Computers and other analytical techniques also became completely integral to every archaeological endeavor. The Kelsey's new projects thus began to include large-scale, systematic regional survey, as well as computer-aided quantifications, graphic presentations, and spatial analysis. The new projects were also informed by fine-tuned and sophisticated research questions, now revolving around such issues as power, ethnicity, contact and exchange, and sacred space. This new age of scholarship, which continues today, is exemplified by projects such as those at Paestum (Italy), Tel Anafa and Kedesh (Israel), Coptos and Abydos (Egypt), Leptiminus (Tunisia), the Pylos Regional Archaeological Project (PRAP) and the Southern Euboea Exploration Project (SEEP), both in Greece, and the Vorotan Project (Armenia).

This booklet, which briefly describes each of the Kelsey Museum's archaeological excavations and surveys since 1924, is offered in memory of Professor Kelsey. It is intended to celebrate both his visionary energy and the numerous archaeological field projects that followed in his wake.

The young Kelsey in a University classroom. Francis W. Kelsey Papers, Bentley Historical Library, University of Michigan.

Map: Locations of Kelsey Museum Fieldwork

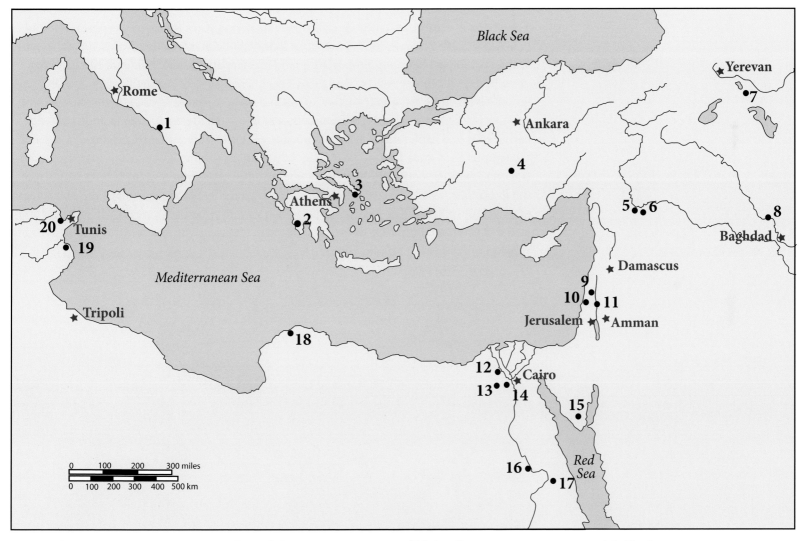

1. Paestum
2. PRAP
3. SEEP
4. Antioch of Pisidia
5. Dibsi Faraj
6. Qasr al-Hayr
7. Vorotan Project
8. Seleucia-on-the-Tigris
9. Kedesh
10. Sepphoris
11. Tel Anafa
12. Terenouthis
13. Soknopaiou Nesos
14. Karanis
15. Monastery of St. Catherine
16. Abydos
17. Coptos
18. Cyrene and Apollonia
19. Leptiminus
20. Carthage

Map

11

David M. Robinson, University of Michigan
Director

Antioch of Pisidia, Turkey
1924

The strategic location of Antioch of Pisidia, on the southern slopes of the Sultan Mountains in central west Turkey, made it an appealing place for many purposes. Around 25 BC, for example, the Roman state founded one of its relatively rare eastern colonies at this site, in part to ensure proper order and military stability in a difficult highland region. In the 1st century AD, St. Paul visited the thriving city of Antioch, using it as one center for his far-flung missionary activities. Such events, recorded in documents ranging from massive inscriptions to the New Testament, attracted the interest of archaeologists. In the early 1900s trial explorations at the site recovered approximately 60 fragments of a copy of the famous *Res Gestae Divi Augusti* (The Achievements of the Divine Augustus), an inscription that commemorated the accomplishments of the first emperor. The bronze original of the *Res Gestae*, which has never been found, was allegedly placed in front of the Mausoleum of Augustus in Rome. The Pisidian copy, which was inscribed in stone and deliberately situated in a prominent position in the ancient town, was clearly meant to extol Augustus to his subjects in the eastern Roman empire.

Workers at the site struggle to tilt up a large inscription. The original inscription consisted of bronze letters; only the holes remain. 7.1123.

The Michigan expedition, which spanned four months in 1924, recovered some 200 additional fragments of this inscription. In the course of tracing its exact placement, the University team also discovered the entrance to a temple area, a large city square, masses of sculptural and architectural fragments, and impressive ruins of Roman and early Christian buildings thought to have been brought down by successive earthquakes. Excavations also recovered an extremely fine white marble portrait head of Augustus, a cast of which now resides in the Kelsey Museum. At the close of the season the staff unearthed a monumental gateway, about 50 meters wide and 13 meters high, in the southwest part of the site. Of equal interest for these early excavators were the remains of a stone aqueduct, its massive arches still intact, which brought plentiful supplies of water to the city for both public and private use. The director, D. M. Robinson, wrote at the time, "Were these monuments in a more accessible place as Rome, for instance, people would come from all over the world to see them."

Apart from Michigan's work at Antioch itself, trial trenches at the nearby site of Sizma revealed heaps of slag, ashes, and refuse from the smelting of cinnabar, in addition to pottery dating to approximately 2500 BC. Robinson suggested that these unusual remains might have represented a prehistoric settlement of miners.

While a second season was scheduled at Antioch, various circumstances prevented the Michigan team from carrying out this plan. Subsequent important work, however, has been performed at the site by archaeologists from Belgium, Canada, Great Britain, and Turkey.

General view of the Tiberia Platea, an open space before a monumental temple. 7.1113.

Antioch of Pisidia, Turkey

Opposite page:

Top: The aqueduct at Antioch. 7.1224.

Bottom left: The head of Augustus coming to light. Enoch Peterson, field director of the Antioch excavations, is second from left in the foreground. KR 54.7.

Bottom right: The head of Augustus, full profile. 7.1258.

Above: Field director Enoch Peterson stands on part of the stone aqueduct that brought water to the city of ancient Antioch. 7.1358.

Below: Block from an Antiochene temple, with sacrificial bull's head and garlands. 5.250.

Archive caption reads: "On August 19, 1924, members of the excavation team embark on a trip to Ankara, Turkey. On this inauspicious day, the 'dig car' gets stuck in the mud [*pictured below*], gas runs dangerously low, and the night in the hotel at Ankara ends with a blazing fire that burns the hotel to the ground." KR 97.2.

J. L. Starkey, University of Michigan
Director, 1924–1925

Enoch E. Peterson, University of Michigan
Director, 1926–1935

Karanis, Egypt

1924–1935

The Graeco-Roman site of Karanis (modern Kom Aushim) is located 80 kilometers southwest of Cairo in the lake district of the Fayoum. One of a number of towns established under Ptolemy II Philadelphus (285–247 BC), Karanis was part of a scheme to settle Greek mercenaries among indigenous populations and to exploit the potential of the fertile Fayoum basin. At its peak Karanis covered over 60 hectares and contained a number of public and commercial buildings, including granaries, military barracks, administrative structures, baths, and two temple complexes. Most structures, however, were private, often multilevel houses. Dated written documents from the site cease in the 5th century AD, but other archaeological finds suggest that the site remained inhabited until the 7th century AD.

Modern interest in the site emerged in the late 1800s when local farmers began to "excavate" the 12-meter-high mound in order to remove its nitrogen-rich soils. These soils, which were the result of decomposing ancient organic debris, served as excellent fertilizers for local crops. Although the activities of the *sebbakhin* (fertilizer diggers) destroyed the central sector of the ancient site, they brought to light an enormous array of archaeological materials. Among the most common finds were ancient papyri—coveted by both private collectors and museums—that regularly surfaced on the antiquities market. The papyri attracted the attention of Professor Francis W. Kelsey, who visited the site in 1920 and decided to rescue Karanis from further destruction. His aims were anything but modest; he hoped that excavations

Below left: Wall painting, of grapes. 5.3850.

Below right: Staff at Karanis, 1926, during Francis Kelsey's (fourth from right) visit to the site. 5.2373.

would help reconstruct the "total environment of life in Graeco-Roman Egypt." Armed with a permit from the Egyptian government, funds from the University of Michigan, and a roster of experts, the University of Michigan team began exploring Karanis during the first few months of 1925. Although Kelsey died in 1927, his team excavated the site for 11 seasons and brought nearly 45,000 objects back to Ann Arbor, all of which are now housed in the Kelsey Museum. The majority of the finds date to the Roman periods of the site.

The strategies adopted at the site were visionary, anticipating by decades methods that would become standard in the archaeological world. The Karanis crew meticulously explored the site room by room, level by level, retaining samples of almost everything they excavated. Nothing was considered insignificant, and the dry climate of Egypt favored remarkable preservation. The Museum's collections include, among other things, food remains, shoes, baskets, rope, mats, textiles, furniture and household fittings, ostraca, glass, sculpture, works of art, papyri, and coins (including a hoard of gold aureii). Images of deities, votives, amulets, and equipment used in religious rites, as well as papyri and inscriptions, suggest that religious practices at Karanis reflected a blend of cultures. Of the 30 deities identified, approximately half belong to the indigenous Egyptian pantheon and half to the list of Graeco-Roman gods and goddesses. Evidence for the rising appeal of Christianity appears late at the site, no earlier than the end of the 3rd century AD.

Taken in aggregate, the remains from Karanis provide an unparalleled window onto the ancient world and allow scholars the unique opportunity to observe in minute detail how daily life was lived by ordinary people nearly 2,000 years ago. The materials housed at the Museum continue to generate scholarly study, ranging from research on textile and glass production to musical instruments and ancient magic.

A view into the passage of House C55C, with a jar sunk into the floor and surrounded by a low wall of brick. 5.2881.

Houses preserved up to three stories in height were not uncommon at Karanis. 5.1928.

Karanis, Egypt

Karanis, Egypt

Opposite page: An impressive view of the excavation in progress. A site supervisor, in a pith helmet, is visible with two workmen through the gap in the house wall. 5.2741

At right: An array of objects from everyday life at Karanis, originally found intact on a windowsill. Photo: Ron Baryash.

Below: In the foreground, one of the largest of Karanis's 17 granaries. 7.2368.

The Tophet

Rev. Père A. Delattre, Honorary Chairman

Francis W. Kelsey, University of Michigan, General Director

Count Byron Khun de Prorok, Associate General Director

1925

The Dermech Site

John G. Pedley, University of Michigan

John Humphrey, University of Michigan

Directors, 1975–1979

The Circus

John Humphrey, University of Michigan

Anne Haeckl, University of Colorado

Naomi Norman, University of Georgia

Directors, 1982–1987

Carthage, Tunisia
1925, 1975–1979, 1982–1987

Beginning in December of 1921, a series of limestone and sandstone stelae with carved symbols associated with the cult of the Punic goddess Tanit appeared on the antiquities market in Tunis, attracting the attention of dignitaries and archaeologists alike to the ruins of ancient Carthage, which lay some 10 kilometers to the north. Having surreptitiously identified the source of these stelae, Count Byron Khun de Prorok purchased the property in 1923 and invited the Abbé Chabot to participate in an exploratory season in 1924. The results were so striking that further excavations were deemed necessary, and Professor Francis W. Kelsey was contacted to serve as general director of the project. The Franco-American team excavated in the sanctuary of Tanit (the Tophet) for three months in the spring of 1925.

The famous site of Carthage, on the coast of modern Tunisia, was founded by the Phoenicians in the 9th century BC, destroyed by Rome in 146 BC during the last Punic War, and later refounded as a Roman colony. Archaeological strata at the site cover the periods from the 8th century BC through the 7th century AD. In one plot, known to be associated with the goddess Tanit and free of modern over-building, the excavators discovered three major strata of inurned infant burials, documented as Tanit I, II, and III. The lowest level of cinerary urns, Tanit

I, was deposited directly on the bedrock, and each urn was surrounded by a small cairn of stones. The urns contained charred bones of young children, lambs, goats, and small birds, as well as rings, bracelets, beads, and objects of gold, silver, and bronze. In Tanit II, the urns were four to five times more numerous, were laid out in roughly aligned rows or discrete groupings, and were frequently marked by a stele. Although Tanit III, the uppermost stratum of burial urns, was badly disturbed by later activity, Kelsey and his team were nevertheless able to reconstruct the density of the urns—approximately six vessels per square meter. A thick layer of burnt earth covering parts of Tanit III was identified as marking the Roman destruction of Punic Carthage in 146 BC.

The Franco-American excavation of the Tophet in Carthage was a model of scientific archaeology as practiced in the early 20th century. The stratigraphic history of the site, based upon the data recovered during the 1925 campaign, remains little changed to this day. The

Opposite page: View over the harbors and the inner part of the Gulf of Tunis, with the local landmark of the "Two-Horned" mountain in the distance. The 1975 excavation at the Dermech was situated at the bottom left-hand corner of the picture. 7.2044.

Below: Excavation in progress in the Tophet, the precinct of Tanit, April 2, 1925. 7.1872.

Carthage, Tunisia

typology constructed for the cinerary urns themselves is also still in use, with only slight refinements. In the years following Kelsey's publication of the site, numerous other Tophets have been identified at Phoenician and Punic sites in the Mediterranean, and the patterns discerned at Carthage have been widely confirmed.

Several Greek and Roman sources tell us that the Tophet at Carthage was the burial place for Punic children sacrificed alive to appease the principal deities of the city, Ba'al and Tanit. Kelsey himself hesitated at such a conclusion: "in our explanation we should resort to the hypothesis of sacrifice of living infants only in case the facts of discovery warrant it; the burden of proof in this instance relies on the affirmative." More recent assessments tend to accept the truth of this, to our eyes, barbaric practice.

Almost five decades after the work of Kelsey and his associates, in 1972 an unprecedented international rescue operation, under the auspices of UNESCO, was inaugurated to save the archaeological heritage of Carthage. The city's remains were at risk from the ever-increasing pace of urbanization associated with the nearby capital city of Tunis. Archaeological teams from France, Germany, Great Britain, Denmark, Poland, Bulgaria, Italy, Sweden, the Netherlands, Canada, and the United States were invited by the Tunisian Institute of Archaeology and Art to participate in this rescue project.

In 1975, the University of Michigan and the Kelsey Museum began archaeological investigations in an area known as Dermech, south of the urban center but within the limits of the Roman city wall. Five seasons of work exposed the remains of an ecclesiastical complex alongside an early Christian basilica, as well as part of a late Roman peristyle house

Below left: A view of cistern tanks at Carthage, photographed in 1925. By the time of the later excavations, the two tanks in the foreground had been filled in. 7.1865.

Below right: Cisterns at Carthage, photographed in 1925. By the time of the later excavations, the terrain around these monuments had been much altered through quarrying and road construction. 7.1866.

(the House of the Greek Charioteers) occupied through the Vandal (5th and early 6th century AD) and Byzantine (mid-6th to mid-7th century AD) periods. The project is notable as the first to undertake a systematic study of Vandal Carthage, a period neglected in the study of the city's long-term history. The Dermech site has been maintained as an archaeological park with a small museum, which houses, among other objects, a remarkable 5th-century statue of Zeus (in the form of an eagle) and Ganymede.

Beginning in 1982, the University of Michigan and the Kelsey Museum sponsored work at the site of the Roman circus in Carthage, at the southern limit of the ancient city. This project was very much a "rescue operation," since unlike the Dermech site, the circus had not been safeguarded during the period of the French Protectorate and had consequently been subject to significant modern development. Building upon the results of a geophysical survey by Polish archaeologists in 1972, the Michigan team was able to clear the area and reconstruct the general shape of the circus arena. In addition to the major architectural phases discerned during excavation, the project was able to elucidate several key questions concerning the role that this public building played in the civic life of late Roman and Byzantine Carthage. Of particular note was the discovery of a series of late intramural burials—a discovery that in turn provided the impetus for several smaller projects investigating the retrenchment of the city in its final phases.

Below left: A view of the Punic ruins at Carthage, today a UNESCO World Heritage Site.
Photo: Jennifer P. Moore.

Below right: Stelae, or gravestones, at the Tophet.
Photo: Jennifer P. Moore.

Carthage, Tunisia

Gemstone of a victorious charioteer, from the circus excavation. Photo: Naomi Norman.

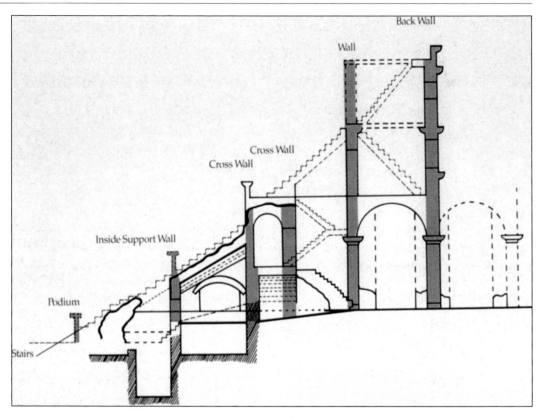

Cross-section of the structure of the Carthage circus. Reconstruction: Naomi Norman.

Near right: Lead curse tablet, impaled by a nail, from the circus excavation. Photo: Naomi Norman.

Far right: Figurine of Aphrodite/Astarte, made of worked bone, from the circus excavation. Photo: Naomi Norman.

Carthage, Tunisia

Statue of Ganymede with Zeus in the guise of an eagle, from the Dermech site.
Photo: Naomi Norman.

Leroy Waterman, University of Michigan
Director, 1927–1932

Robert H. McDowell, University of Michigan
Field Director, 1930–1931

Clark Hopkins, University of Michigan
Director, 1936–1937

Robert H. McDowell, University of Michigan
Field Director, 1936–1937

Seleucia-on-the-Tigris, Iraq
1927–1932, 1936–1937

The ancient city of Seleucia, 35 kilometers south of modern Baghdad, Iraq, was a political center of the Seleucid empire. One of several cities established to consolidate the power of Alexander the Great's successors, it was founded by the general Seleucus Nicator, whose share of Alexander's empire stretched from the Mediterranean to India. By virtue of its location at one of the narrowest points between the Tigris and the Euphrates, and along a well-traveled caravan route leading from Syria to central Asia, Seleucia controlled some of the major routes of communication in the ancient world.

Seleucia lost its imperial standing in 141 BC when it was conquered by the Iranian-based Parthian empire, and the Seleucid kingdom retreated to its western capital at Antioch-on-the-Orontes. Nonetheless, the city retained a cosmopolitan character until its eventual abandonment at the end of the Parthian period, around AD 200.

The University of Michigan excavated Seleucia, modern Tell Umar, for six seasons between 1927 and 1937. Among the most innovative aspects of the work was the use of aerial photography, in one of its first systematic applications to archaeology. This project

The excavation in progress, December 1929. Seleucia Photo Archive c149.

was undertaken with help from the British Royal Air Force, then stationed in Baghdad. The excavations were led by Leroy Waterman and, after the Depression, by Clark Hopkins, on behalf of the American School of Oriental Research of Baghdad, with funds supplied by the University of Michigan, the Toledo Museum of Art, and the Cleveland Museum of Art.

The Michigan excavations established the general outlines of the city and revealed that it was laid out on a grid plan. A canal running through the center seemed to divide the city into two parts: a largely public northern sector and a residential area in the south. During the Seleucid period, the southern sector housed private and official archives, large residential shops on the street facades, and rooms of varying size arranged around courtyards. Burial practices and the extensive remains of terracotta figurines exhibit both Greek (Hellenistic) and Near Eastern elements, suggesting that throughout its existence the city accommodated Greek settlers as well as a more indigenous population. Later excavations by the University of Torino in Italy uncovered a large and impressive archive that provides valuable evidence on Seleucid administration and economy.

The Kelsey Museum now houses approximately 12,000 objects unearthed at this site, including one of the largest collections of Parthian pottery to be found outside of Iraq.

The Seleucia team, with dog.
Seleucia Photo Archive #1.

Top: A general view of an area designated Block B, Level III (occupation dated to 142 BC– AD 43), taken in November 1931. Seleucia Photo Archive f13.

Bottom: View south over a residential court in Level III, taken in November 1931. Seleucia Photo Archive e35.

Pottery assemblage in situ.
Seleucia Photo Archive d295.

Grave vault found in Trial Trench 18, 1929–1930.
Seleucia Photo Archive c71.

Leroy Waterman, University of Michigan
Director

Sepphoris, Israel
1931

Ancient Sepphoris—known as Zippori in Hebrew, previously the Arab village of Suffuriyye—was excavated for one brief season in 1931. Leroy Waterman, professor of Semitic Languages at the University of Michigan, selected the site because of its renown in the development of both rabbinic Judaism and Christianity: the Mishnah (the tract of Jewish law) was encoded there, and tradition held that Sepphoris was both the home of Jesus's grandparents and the site of the Annunciation. Situated 6.4 kilometers northwest of Nazareth, on a rocky mound above the adjoining plains, the site boasted a long history of occupation, spanning from at least the 3rd century BC until the Crusades.

Although survey and excavation by Waterman's team lasted only two short months, impressive remains were recovered. The survey team traced and documented the city's water system, including a portion of the Roman aqueduct and an enormous underground reservoir as well as a series of ancient tombs. Excavation exposed a large Roman theater that seated 4,000 to 5,000 people—the first of its kind recorded for a city in ancient Palestine—and a substantial building that was believed at the time to be a Christian basilica, but is now considered to be the ruins of a Roman villa.

In the 1970s several universities in America and Israel resumed investigation of this promising site. Excavations continue today, and Sepphoris is now part of a national preserve, Zippori National Park. Recent discoveries of exquisite mosaics, wealthy villas, and a synagogue have brought Sepphoris international attention as a city whose multicultural population included Jews, Christians, pagans, and, later, Arabs. In 1995 the citadel on the upper city was converted into a museum. One of the rooms is dedicated to the history of the site's early excavations, where some 40 objects on long-term loan from the Kelsey Museum are now on display. These include various domestic utensils, such as cooking pots and tools for carpentry and weaving, as well as toys, beads, and lamps.

Below: The director's room in the expedition house; "where I spent one third of my time," Waterman remarked. Sepphoris Photo Archive 17.

Below right: Expedition "water wagon" (capacity 40 gallons), which provided daily water for the workmen. Sepphoris Photo Archive 104.

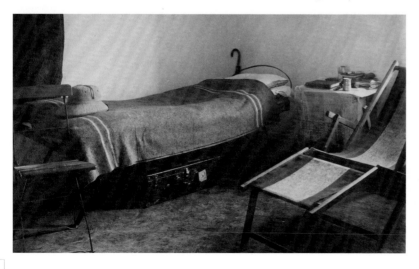

Group photograph of the project workmen. Sepporhis Photo Archive 72.

Seats in the Roman theater. Sepphoris Photo Archive 75.

General view of work conducted beneath the "Crusader" citadel. The citadel served as the village school, so that excavation could only be carried out during the school's summer vacation. Today the citadel serves as a museum. Sepphoris Photo Archive 18.

Sepphoris, Israel

Enoch E. Peterson, University of Michigan
Director

Soknopaiou Nesos (Dimé), Egypt
1931–1932

Concurrent with the campaigns at Karanis (1924–35), Enoch E. Peterson, director of the Karanis project as well as of the Kelsey Museum, led preliminary expeditions to two other sites: Soknopaiou Nesos, modern Dimé (or Dimai), and Terenouthis, modern Kom Abou Billou.

For part of the 1931–32 season, the University of Michigan team temporarily suspended its work at Karanis and shifted its activities to the nearby Hellenistic-Roman site of Soknopaiou Nesos, also in the Fayoum. The motivation for the shift was twofold: first to compare the chronology worked out for the various levels at Karanis with those of a contemporary site in the region and, second, to find a new site that would warrant excavation after work at Karanis had concluded.

Like other neighboring sites, Soknopaiou Nesos had been plundered for papyri and antiquities, and the central portion of the mound was largely destroyed. Despite modern

Trap door entrance to one of two secret chambers in a private house or public structure. The chamber consisted of a hollow space approximately 2 meters deep. The wooden trap door was concealed by a layer of floor bricks. 5.3873.

View of Soknopaiou Nesos, with the dump cart used to transport the excavated soil. 5.3864.

damage, the site yielded interesting traces of houses, as well as a small but valuable collection of coins, Greek inscriptions, and customs seals and receipts. Previous excavations had already exposed a temple to the god the Greeks called Sobek, the crocodile god of the Fayoum. The town appears to have been a "frontier" settlement, occupied from approximately 240 BC until the 2nd century AD. Although generally prosperous, it witnessed periods of decline and perhaps partial abandonment during its history.

Plans to launch full-scale exploration of the site were never seriously pursued. The difficulties encountered by the excavators during the 1931–32 season dissuaded them from future work. As one investigator wrote: "There is no water of any sort available at [Dimai] itself and the water of the adjacent . . . lake is quite unfit for use. . . . The restriction thus imposed upon our supplies of water and food necessarily limited the use of our working force. Fewer than one hundred men and boys could be maintained at [Dimai], in contrast to the much larger numbers customary at [Karanis]."

Wall painting in one of the houses. The image is interpreted as a cult scene, with the owner of the house and his wife in the act of making an offering to Soknopaios, a form of the Egyptian god Sobek. 5.3887.

House I-108 during excavation. Houses were often arranged in blocks around courtyards, which were used for milling, baking, and stabling livestock. 5.3920.

Soknopaiou Nesos (Dimê), Egypt

Enoch E. Peterson, University of Michigan
Director

Terenouthis, Egypt
1935

An ancient necropolis, Terenouthis is located on the edge of the western desert, approximately 65 kilometers northwest of Cairo. In antiquity, the site stood out as a large mound probably given over entirely to burial purposes. By the time the University of Michigan began its excavations, however, only a small zone in the mound's southeast corner had been spared destruction by the modern *sebbakhin*, or fertilizer diggers. Excavation in this approximately 500-square-meter area was further hampered by the presence of the Egyptian Salt and Soda Company's Decauville line, which ran along the mound's southern side. This company transported natural salt mined in the desert a short distance from the site.

Despite these limitations, the excavators recovered more than 200 tombs and stelae dating from the Middle Kingdom through late Roman times, the bulk of which date from the late 3rd and early 4th centuries AD. The tombs were built of mudbrick, and each contained an arched niche, usually on the eastern side of the tomb. A stele was placed against the back wall of the niche, and occasionally a sacrificial altar stood in front of the tomb.

Human interments were most often found between tombs, and coins recovered in burials provided firm evidence for dating. Coins were placed in the hands of the deceased, beneath the skull, or carefully arranged on top of the corpse in rows from chin to abdomen.

Although rudimentary in style, the iconography on the stelae reflects a telling syncretism, combining older Egyptian symbols with Greek and Roman artistic traditions. As one researcher observed, the combination of these traditions "in a workable compromise . . . was well suited to meet the demands of a mixed population." Inscriptions on the stelae also enlighten us on life expectancy: the average age of death for those who survived childhood was 28 years for women and 37 for men.

Opposite page, top left: Painted tomb with antithetically placed jackals representing Anubis, the Egyptian god of the dead. 580.

Opposite page, bottom left: Unusual human burial found between two tombs. The burial was that of a woman, wrapped, covered with plaster, and colored primarily with red and black pigments. 5.4410.

Below: Funerary stele with standing woman in a shrine. KM 2.1055.

Below right: Two mudbrick painted tombs with niches, painted stelae, and an altar in front of the tombs. 5.4346.

Top right: Painted niche: Anubis, Egyptian god of the dead. KM 2.9015.

Bottom right: Painted niche: A deceased woman, reclining and holding out a drinking vessel. KM 2.9014.

George H. Forsyth, Jr.,
University of Michigan
Field Director 1958, 1960

Kurt Weitzmann, Princeton University
Field Director 1963, 1965

Images reproduced through the courtesy
of the Michigan-Princeton-Alexandria
Expeditions to Mount Sinai.

Below: Fred Anderegg photographing the mosaics of
the church at the monastery. Photo: G. Forsyth.

Below right: George Forsyth being assisted by local
Bedouins with his survey of the foundations of the
monastery. Photo: F. Anderegg.

Monastery of St. Catherine at Mount Sinai, Egypt
(with Princeton University and the University of Alexandria)
1958, 1960, 1963, 1965

In 1956 the University of Michigan sent a reconnaissance expedition under the direction of George Forsyth to survey archaeological sites in the Near East. The stay at Mount Sinai led to the collaboration that followed, first and chiefly with Princeton University (Professor Kurt Weitzmann) and, later, the University of Alexandria (Professor Ahmed Fikry). The still-active, 6th-century monastery of St. Catherine at Sinai's Mount of Moses is an isolated stronghold the size of a city block. Despite its wilderness setting, the large fortress preserves remarkable Byzantine treasures, including brilliant wall mosaics, encaustic mural paintings, and an impressively substantial collection of icons and manuscripts. With an international team of scholars joining the Michigan enterprise, full-scale campaigns were undertaken in 1958, 1960, 1963, and 1965. The aim was to create a comprehensive record of the monastery's architecture, sculptures, decorative arts, and paintings, including its highly renowned icons. Despite formidable difficulties presented by the remote and barren location of the site, technical facilities were established at the monastery, including installation of a photographic laboratory, elaborate scaffolding, and surveying equipment. The monastic community provided a friendly reception critical to the success of the enterprise. The four campaigns of

research, study, and photography yielded a wealth of information that continues to provide invaluable documentation for scholars. Under the direction of Professor Forsyth, then chairman of the Department of the History of Art and later director of the Kelsey Museum, the architectural survey was completed, and the first large-scale scientific drawings of the church and monastery were prepared for publication.

The Byzantine emperor Justinian I had the granite monastery built as a fortress that sheltered a community of monks and also marked the traditional sacred site of the Burning Bush of Moses, near the base of the mountain. With amazing longevity, the monastery's church has undergone few changes since its erection in the 6th century. The building is intact. Its western portal is still closed by its original, beautifully carved wood doors. Despite being over 1,400 years old, they need only a slight nudge to function perfectly in their first pins and hinges. The original wood roof over the nave of the church rests on carved 6th-century beams that are inscribed with prayers honoring Justinian and his famous wife, Theodora. The wording of these inscriptions (urging salvation for "our most pious Emperor," the living Justinian, and his "late Empress" Theodora) indicates that construction of the church can be reliably dated between the deaths of Theodora in 548 and of Justinian in 565. The inscriptions also name the "architect," Stephanos of Aila.

When first encountered, the church's splendid gold wall mosaics, which sheath the apse above the high altar, were partially in danger of collapse. Ernest Hawkins (of the Byzantine Institute and Dumbarton Oaks) was called from Istanbul to direct their consolidation and cleaning. He carried this out in 1959, restoring their original brilliance.

Members of the 1963 Michigan-Princeton-Alexandria Expeditions with some of the monks in the Monastery of St. Catherine. Photo: F. Anderegg.

The mosaics illustrate Moses in scenes from both the Old Testament (Moses receiving the Tables of the Law and Moses at the Burning Bush) and the New Testament (the Transfiguration on Mount Tabor with Moses and Elijah framing the transfigured Christ and his disciples). Conscious of the uniqueness of its important artistic heritage, the monastic community at Sinai has recently made renewed efforts to conserve these extraordinary works. Brought to the attention of the scholarly public by the Michigan-Princeton-Alexandria Expeditions, these singular mosaics are believed by experts to exceed in quality and condition others from Justinian's time that are still known in the Mediterranean world.

Publication of the work of the Expeditions continues. In addition to articles in scholarly journals, several volumes under the series title *The Monastery of Saint Catherine at Mount Sinai* have appeared.

The Church of St. Catherine, Mount Sinai,
interior of the nave. Photo: F. Anderegg.

Distant view of the Monastery of St. Catherine, Mount Sinai. Photo: G. Forsyth.

Oleg Grabar, University of Michigan
Director

Qasr al-Hayr al-Sharqi, Syria

1964, 1966, 1969–1971

Qasr al-Hayr al-Sharqi sits at the foot of one of the few mountain passes in the central Syrian desert, a forbidding, steppe-like region that is amenable to agriculture only through periodic rains and irrigation. An important medieval Islamic town, the site commanded a strategic position between settled and nomadic groups. The spectacular remains, which were built over the course of a 75-year period, consisted of an outer wall nearly 20 kilometers long and approximately 12 meters tall in places, several round towers, four main gates, two enclosures, a mosque, olive presses, a large bath, an elaborate system of canals and water controls, and an area for agriculture and animal husbandry.

Although archaeologists knew that the site had been occupied for many centuries, its founding and precise dates of habitation were unknown. Equally vexing, these impressive remains seemed an anomaly to scholars: they fit neither the traditional notion of Roman settlement during the empire nor the pattern of nomadic sites, which were usually devoid of monumental architecture. Before excavations were undertaken, the site was most often recorded in the literature as a Roman military outpost that saw extensive later reuse. A French traveler, who visited the site in 1808, however, recovered an inscription (now lost) that began to alter that perception. Discovered in a mosque within the enclosure, the inscription commemorated the founding of a city in AD 728–729 by order of one of the most powerful rulers of the first Islamic dynasty, the Umayyads. Although the Roman designation prevailed in the minds of scholars for many years, the site gradually began to be seen as an early Islamic palace, founded at the edges of the desert.

Panoramic photo of the façade of the small enclosure. Qasr al-Hayr Photo Archive #1.panoramic.

The evidence uncovered by the University's excavations finally clarified the purpose and dates of the site. Qasr al-Hayr was indeed founded in the early Islamic period. It was not, however, in the words of the director, a "princely pleasure palace" but instead an aristocratic settlement and *Khan*—a trade enclosure of monumental proportions, with six nearly identical residences. The stout outer walls enclose an administrative and aristocratic living center whose heyday came in the middle of the 8th century. The center declined and was partially destroyed by fires in the 10th century, experienced a kind of renaissance in the 12th century (when the ruins of the early settlement were reused for a modest urban center), and was finally abandoned in the 14th century. Thereafter the site seems to have served only as a temporary shelter in the desert.

Qasr al-Hayr is now viewed as part of an important and emerging frontier zone within the Syrian desert during the early years of Muslim rule; the fact that it was not extensively reoccupied or reconfigured makes it a special prize for Islamic scholars. The immense wealth amassed by the Umayyad dynasty, whose powerful reach included Spain, India, and the frontiers of China, enabled them to invest lavishly in sites such as Qasr al-Hayr. The archaeological surveys and excavations mounted by the director of the project uncovered nearly 32 kilometers of underground canals, a sign not only of great expenditure but also a substantial command of labor. Qasr al-Hayr represents a huge investment of time and money, and it carefully orchestrated social and commercial relationships between nomadic and settled life in an area that had long been viewed as inhospitable.

A photo of the excavation dig house humorously labeled in the excavation scrapbook "Bed and Breakfast at the Taibi Hilton." Qasr al-Hayr Photo Archive 1964i9.

Opposite page: An early aerial photo of Qasr al-Hayr al-Sharqi. The two enclosures formed the urban focus within a larger walled area. One end of the walled area contained structures for controlling waters from seasonal flash floods. Qasr al-Hayr Photo Archive #64.

At right: Local workers. Qasr al-Hayr Photo Archive 1966M8.

Below right: Visiting a nearby spring. Qasr al-Hayr Photo Archive 1964e16.

Apollonia
Clark Hopkins, University of Michigan
Director, 1965

John G. Pedley and Donald White,
University of Michigan
Directors, 1966–1967

Cyrene
Donald White, University of Michigan
Director, 1969, 1971

Donald White, University of Pennsylvania
Director, 1973–1981

Below: Excavation in progress in the area of the sea gate, Apollonia. Apollonia Photo Archive 65-j-108.

Below right: The project architect at work at Apollonia. Apollonia Photo Archive 67-162.

Apollonia, Libya
1965–1967

Cyrene, Libya
1969, 1971, 1973–1981

The neighboring sites of Apollonia and Cyrene share a similar history, both being occupied for approximately 1,000 years and both recognized in Roman times as major cities in the Libyan Pentapolis (Region of the Five Cities). Cyrene was originally settled by Greeks around the end of the 7th century BC, and Apollonia served as its port for many centuries.

The initial excavations carried out by the University of Michigan at Apollonia concentrated on the area of the sea gate, including underwater investigation of the extensive but now sunken harbor installations. Later excavations focused on an "unknown structure" within the city walls that turned out to be an elaborate, unfinished bathing establishment dating to late Roman times. About one kilometer west of the city wall members of the Apollonia expedition also uncovered remains of a Doric temple that was in danger of being consumed by urban sprawl and the modern dump. Also visible at the site today is a well-preserved theater and several churches.

The University of Michigan's involvement at Cyrene was the result of a happy accident. In the spring of 1966, while University archaeologists were digging at Apollonia, the Libyan government was constructing houses in what was intended to be the new village of Shahat—modern Cyrene. In the process of digging foundations for the new village, construction

workers discovered remains of an ancient aqueduct, a number of bronze items, and several stone statues. The archaeologists working at Apollonia were called in, and after some preliminary investigations, the extramural Sanctuary of Demeter and Persephone began to be excavated in 1969. Sponsorship of the site later shifted to the University of Pennsylvania when the director, Donald White, joined Pennsylvania's Museum of Archaeology and Anthropology. In 1981, after seven seasons of excavation and two study seasons, fieldwork ended.

Famous in antiquity for its horses, cereals, vines, olives, and silphium (a highly sought-after plant known for its medicinal properties), Cyrene supported a prosperous elite. The substantial wealth of the city financed splendid buildings, baths, a theater, and two sanctuaries, one to Apollo, the other to Demeter and Persephone (mother-daughter goddesses intertwined with the cycle of life and death, vegetation, and fertility).

The Sanctuary of Demeter and Persephone, which formed the focus of the Michigan excavations, was founded ca. 600 BC and visited by worshippers until badly damaged by a severe earthquake in AD 262. The sanctuary was totally destroyed by an even more disastrous earthquake in AD 365. The impressive complex covered more than 9,000 square meters, distributed over 20 meters of abruptly rising ground and reached by several sets of stairs and a bridge. Excavations unearthed a mass of votive deposits from the earlier use of the sanctuary (including pottery, lamps, stone and terracotta figurines and statuettes, gems, seals, jewelry, glass containers, and utensils) in addition to a series of fine, nearly life-size and life-size statues of Hellenistic and Roman imperial date, some possibly representing cult statues of Persephone and Demeter.

Below left: Plunge tank within the late Roman baths, Apollonia. Apollonia Photo Archive 67-23.

Below right: The theater at Apollonia. Apollonia Photo Archive 67-54.

Apollonia and Cyrene, Libya

Opposite page:

Left: Excavation of the Sanctuary of Demeter and Persephone in progress, with a photographic tripod being erected. Cyrene Photo Archive.

Right: As assemblage of the baskets used at Cyrene to move earth and to contain artifactual finds; note the attached labels indicating the material's specific archaeological context. Cyrene Photo Archive.

This page:

Near right: Workmen preparing to remove a large column, Sanctuary of Demeter and Persephone. Cyrene Photo Archive.

Far right: Draped torso of a woman (or goddess?) found at the Sanctuary of Demeter and Persephone. Cyrene Photo Archive.

Below left: Conservation work in progress on finds from the Sanctuary of Demeter and Persephone. Cyrene Photo Archive.

Below right: Head of a goddess, from the Sanctuary of Demeter and Persephone. Cyrene Photo Archive.

Saul S. Weinberg, University of Missouri
Director 1968–1973

Sharon C. Herbert, University of Michigan
Director 1978–1986

Photos courtesy of Sharon C. Herbert

Tel Anafa, Israel
1968–1973, 1978–1986

Tel Anafa lies at the foot of the Golan Heights in the Upper Galilee of modern Israel, in sight of both the Lebanese and Syrian borders. Ten seasons of excavation by teams from the Kelsey Museum and the University of Missouri Museum of Art and Archaeology revealed remains of a rich and remarkably well-preserved Hellenistic settlement, as well as evidence for almost continuous occupation at the site from the Early Bronze Age through the early Roman period. Study of this evidence allows us to begin to unravel the complex tapestry of changing lifeways in this volatile part of the ancient Near East and to shed light on the workings of the social and economic networks in which the inhabitants of the tel and their neighbors participated.

Remains from the late Hellenistic era (150–75 BC) have proven most informative. During those years the site appears to have served as the country estate of affluent citizens from nearby Tyre. These wealthy residents decorated their palatial villa in the latest Greek style and furnished it with all available luxuries, including fine tablewares and thousands of expensive glass drinking vessels. True to their Phoenician heritage, they paid particular attention to comfortable private bathing facilities within the house. The richness of the finds,

View of Tel Anafa surrounded by the cotton fields of Kibbutz Shamir.

coupled with the clear chronological context and careful recording techniques employed by the excavators, have made Tel Anafa extremely valuable to all those interested in the Hellenistic world. Indeed, for many bodies of Hellenistic material, Tel Anafa serves as a typological and chronological "type site," presenting a broader and more closely dated range of ceramic forms than ever before possible.

Beyond typology and chronology, issues of the extent of cultural and ethnic diversity within the Hellenistic world can be addressed through the study of the remains from Tel Anafa. The years of the site's greatest prosperity (125–75 BC) were those when the Greek-dominated Seleucid empire was crumbling. For the brief time until Roman armies reestablished foreign domination of the Levant, Graeco-Phoenician citizens of nearby Tyre and Sidon controlled the area and profited greatly from the established Seleucid trade networks. The late Hellenistic settlement at Tel Anafa was a product of this Graeco-Phoenician environment, with a complex interplay between these two elements. Accidents of archaeological preservation and modern political realities make it one of the very few such sites accessible for excavation. Tel Anafa offers, then, a rare opportunity to study Greek culture in direct contact with Phoenician. The archaeological contribution to our understanding of this phenomenon is particularly important since the written sources are almost exclusively Greek, and it is only in the archaeological record that the Phoenician elements receive "equal billing." The evidence from Tel Anafa will enhance understanding of both the "Classical" and "Oriental" components of Hellenistic civilization, underlining the diversity of Western society's heritage from the ancient world.

Bronze head of the god Pan from a decorative headrest. Hellenistic period.

Far left: Sieving for botanical remains, which provide evidence for both diet and agricultural activity at the site.

Near left top: Fragments of Hellenistic glass.

Near left bottom: Hellenistic coins of bronze and silver.

Opposite page:

Left: Excavation of a Roman house pavement, above the southwest corner of the Hellenistic courtyard, 1979.

Top right: Reconstruction of central room of bath with wall paintings above the basin. Drawing: D. W. Reynolds.

Bottom right: Bronze Age pavement beneath the remains of Roman and Hellenistic houses. The highest step in the far distance represents the Roman remains; the next step down shows the Hellenistic layer.

This page:

Top left: Michigan students, in 1980, excavating a deposit of Hellenistic fine wares in the colonnade outside the Hellenistic bath complex.

Top right: The Kelsey Museum conservator mending pottery from this same deposit excavated in 1980.

Bottom: The restored Hellenistic fine wares.

Tel Anafa, Israel

51

Richard Harper, University of Michigan
Director

Images reproduced from Richard Harper
(with an appendix by Tony J. Wilkinson),
"Excavations at Dibsi Faraj, Northern
Syria, 1972–1974: A Preliminary Note on
the Site and Its Monuments," *Dumbarton
Oaks Papers* 29 (1975): 319–38. Dumbarton Oaks, Trustees for Harvard University; used by permission.

Opposite page

Top: Aerial view of the 5th-century AD basilica. Harper 1975: plate 11.

Bottom left: Caldarium (hot room) of the baths inside the walls. Harper 1975: plate 6a.

Bottom right: Animal hunt mosaic from the frigidarium (cooling room) of the extramural baths. Harper 1975: plate 7b.

Dibsi Faraj, Syria

1972–1974

The large and long-lived settlement of Dibsi Faraj in northern Syria is today inundated by a reservoir (Lake Assad) created by the construction of the Tabqa Dam in 1974. Shortly before the area was scheduled for flooding, however, survey teams from the Kelsey Museum and the Dumbarton Oaks Center for Byzantine Studies were invited by Syria's Department of Antiquities to explore the region for locations that might prove interesting to both institutions. The modern site of Dibsi Faraj was selected as promising: the unexcavated but still visible remains were extensive, and the site occupied a naturally defensible location with access to a fertile riverine flood plain and seasonal grazing areas.

Only general details were known about the history of this fortified urban settlement before excavation. Even its ancient name was a matter of debate. Epigraphic evidence suggested that its name likely altered over the course of its long history, changing from Roman Athis, to late Roman and early Byzantine Neocaesarea, and finally to early Islamic Qasrin.

Aerial view of the major building complex. Harper 1975: plate 4a.

While that debate still continues, it is clear that the site supported at least ten centuries of domestic and military occupation, from the beginning of the 1st century AD to the end of the 10th century AD.

Excavations revealed an economically flourishing and robust settlement that underwent several transformations, now identified with at least three main phases. The first phase consisted of a small (unfortified) Roman settlement founded in the early 1st century and located on the west part of the citadel. The second phase began in the late 3rd century AD, when the entire citadel area, some 5 hectares in extent, was surrounded by a circuit wall. Structures within the walls included remains of a garrison, military headquarters, and possibly the home of a local Roman commander. Occupation was not, however, confined to areas within the walls. The community extended over a large extramural area, of some 20 hectares, that was defended by a bank and earthworks. The settlement was clearly expanding during this phase, and by the 4th century a public bath and basilica (with an inscription dating to AD 429) were completed. The third and last phase of the site was assigned to the early Byzantine empire, when extensive reconstruction of the circuit wall was undertaken.

Dibsi Faraj remains one of the few "fortress cities" of the Near East that provides good archaeological evidence for its overall trajectory of development. Indeed, it may be typical of other comparable sites for which there is only limited information. These communities probably began as small settlements without city status in the Roman world, but were later provided with defenses against the increasing Persian penetration of the Euphrates Valley, as well as with increasingly elaborate facilities and extramural civilian housing—all of which enhanced their status within the large and sprawling Roman empire. As successful military colonies, they continued to survive and were refortified and often modified in the early Byzantine period.

Dibsi Faraj, Syria

John G. Pedley, University of Michigan
Mario Torelli, University of Perugia
Directors, 1981–1986

John G. Pedley, University of Michigan
James Higginbotham, Bowdoin College
Directors, 1995–1998

Paestum-Poseidonia, Italy
1981–1986, 1995–1998

Paestum, the ancient Greek Poseidonia, is one of the better preserved classical cities of the ancient world. Located approximately 80 kilometers south of Naples, the site is renowned for its fine complex of Greek temples. Founded by Greeks at the end of the 7th century BC, the town became a Roman colony in 273 BC. The later remains of the Roman town include a forum, houses, baths, and streets.

Michigan's efforts concentrated in an area outside the city walls known as the *località Santa Venera*. The sector had been the focus of sporadic explorations in the 19th century, then in 1951 (prompted by the extension of a tomato paste factory), and again in 1974. This work produced significant quantities of terracotta figurines, architectural and sculptural fragments, and traces of several buildings, some of which were generally agreed to constitute an extramural sanctuary. The identity of the deity worshipped at the site, however,

General view of the 1990s excavations and "stoa'" from the east. Photo: J. G. Pedley..

remained unclear. An intriguing fragmentary inscription suggested that, in the Roman period at least, the divinity worshipped may have been Bona Dea, a goddess associated with a significant mystery cult about which little was known. Armed with questions about the architectural and cultic history of the buildings, teams from the Kelsey Museum and the University of Perugia began excavations in the early 1980s.

These excavations were able to establish a reliable if complex sequence for the architectural phasing of several buildings and to confirm that the site was actively in use for nearly 1,000 years, from the 6th century BC through the 3rd century AD. The main buildings included an Oikos (a type of religious building, usually rectangular in plan, without columns and with a single entrance), an adjacent Rectangular Hall, and a Piscina (pool) in front of the Rectangular Hall. The Oikos and Rectangular Hall were used and rebuilt several times during the Greek and Roman eras, while the Piscina was a Roman elaboration of 1st-century date.

The Oikos was probably the scene of sacrifice and related ceremony. The large Rectangular Hall contained a deposit of bird bones and votive objects during its Greek phase, suggestive of sacrifice and dining. Replanned in Roman times, the hall saw the addition of several unusual niches. While the precise function of these niches is not known, the excavators speculate that at least one possibility includes the use of the building as a kind of "Hall of Initiation." Statues or other religious paraphernalia may have remained hidden in the niches, to be revealed to devotees as time and circumstances decreed. The Piscina, or fishpond, reminds us that in other sanctuaries of the Greek world (e.g., at Samothrace) fish were regarded as sacred. Doubtless this was the case in the Santa Venera sanctuary, where an inscription has confirmed that the deity worshipped was Venus (with Aphrodite her predecessor during the Greek phase of the city's life).

In the 1990s excavations were carried out in an adjacent field, west of the Aphrodite sanctuary, where tombs of the Roman period were examined. No fewer than 18 burials were studied, ranging in date between the late 1st and early 3rd centuries of our era. Stone-lined cists covered with stone or roof tiles were used for the adults, while children were placed in wooden coffins or ceramic vessels. Excavation in this necropolis also revealed strata associated with an earlier Greek occupation. Beginning in 1997, study focused on an area where the remains of an archaic Greek building connected to cult practice were uncovered. The remains of limestone ashlar walls and sand foundations profile a rectangular building with the overall dimensions of approximately 10.3 × 13 meters. Excavations also suggest the general design of the structure, with a long narrow area (portico) facing the east and three rooms, side by side, at the rear. Unexpected finds include two votive Doric capitals (one remarkably preserved with the original paint) placed within the sand foundations of the building. Pottery and bones found within the building attest to frequent banqueting; and some of the vessels bear inscribed dedications. These include the earliest instance of writing in Greek yet found at Paestum-Poseidonia. It is now believed that the building's design and apparent function fit that of a stoa or portico that formed part of a larger sanctuary. Worshippers probably retired here to celebrate the fruits of religious rites and enjoy their portions of the sacrifices. Exact identification of the deity honored at the stoa awaits further research.

Two views of a Roman "capanna-type" tomb with gable intact (top) and skeleton inside (bottom). Photo: J. Higginbotham.

Above left: Photographing a preserved stretch of floor of the Dining Hall in its Greek phase.
Photo: J. G. Pedley.

Above right: Measuring and drawing excavated features. Photo: J. G. Pedley.

Unraveling the strata in the Rectangular Hall.
Photo: J. G. Pedley.

Two Italian team members enjoy a break. Photo: J. G. Pedley.

Italian and American team members with Museum and Superintendency staff at an end of season alfresco event. Photo: J. G. Pedley.

Top: Fragments of an Ionian cup with painted inscription. Photo: J. Higginbotham.

Middle: At upper right, two Doric capitals in situ, placed upright and reused to line the foundation of the late archaic building. Photo: J. Higginbotham.

Bottom: Votive Doric capital, limestone with paint. Photo: J. G. Pedley.

Sharon C. Herbert, University of Michigan

Henry T. Wright, University of Michigan

Directors

Photos courtesy of Sharon C. Herbert

Coptos and the Eastern Desert, Egypt

1987–1995

This project was designed to document the earliest interaction between the Mediterranean and South Asia, when traders from the Ptolemaic kingdom of Hellenistic Egypt (323–33 BC) opened routes from the Nile Valley, across the Eastern Desert, down the Red Sea, and over the Indian Ocean to South Asia. The Michigan team focused on surveying and dating the fortified campsites in the Eastern Desert that provided the infrastructure for the overland leg of this route.

Excavations were also undertaken at the cosmopolitan city of Coptos, the transshipment point at the juncture of the Nile and the desert routes, to provide a stratified sequence of local ceramics, which, analyzed in conjunction with finds from the fortified stations in the Eastern Desert, would allow close dating and better understanding of the Graeco-Roman trade routes to the Red Sea. Excavation was conducted at Coptos in four seasons from 1987 to 1992; survey took place in the Eastern Desert in the winters of 1987, 1988/89, and

The archaeological zone on Qift's weekly market day.

Coptos and the Eastern Desert, Egypt

1990/91, and in conjunction with study seasons in the winters of 1993/94 and 1994/95. The survey and excavation teams worked in tandem, sharing personnel and resources. The project was designed in cooperation with, and overseen in Egypt by, Ahmad El-Sawy of the Sohag branch of Assiut University.

Coptos lies on the east bank of the Nile, 38 kilometers northeast of Luxor. Inhabited from at least the Early Dynastic period (third millennium BC) to the present, it was the capital of the fifth, or Coptite, nome of Upper Egypt. Its location at the point of the Nile closest to the Red Sea made it from earliest times an important trade center and gateway to the mineral resources of the Eastern Desert. Today the greater part of the site lies under the growing market town of Qift, which encircles ancient Coptos and is encroaching upon the numerous, but diminishing, exposed archaeological remains. The protected archaeological zone serves as the municipal dump. Consequently, the site presents something of a depressing lunar landscape with isolated pillars of preserved antiquities surrounded by modern apartment buildings, cut through by modern roads, and inhabited by herds of goats and packs of feral dogs living off the garbage deposited daily. In recent years the Supreme Council of Antiquities has made serious efforts to preserve parts of the site, but it remains in danger of disappearing entirely.

The University of Michigan/University of Assiut team excavated at Coptos from 1987 to 1992 in largely Ptolemaic-Roman levels to the north and east of the Min temple uncovered

Area of Hellenistic houses at Coptos, from the east, before excavation in 1990.

by Sir William Flinders Petrie in his 1893 work at the site. Stratified deposits ranging in date from the Middle Kingdom to the 5th century AD were recovered and, after some years of study, published in 2003. Evidence to date the eastern wall of the *temenos* (sacred precinct) to the reign of Nectanebo I or II (4th century BC) was discovered, as well as a sequence of early Hellenistic houses within the *temenos*. Remains of a later (mid-2nd century BC) *temenos* wall, supplanting that of Nectanebo, were found to the north of the temple. Interestingly, the room in the northeast angle of this wall was decorated by painted stucco in Macedonian style imitating carved stone blocks.

The Michigan/Assiut excavations at Coptos recovered more than 5,000 kilograms of pottery, the great bulk of which is found in stratified contexts of Hellenistic or Roman date,

Below left : Excavated section showing the 4 meters of stratified debris deposited in the area of the Hellenistic houses from the 4th to the 1st centuries BC.

Below right: Area of the Hellenistic houses, from the north, at completion of the excavation in June 1992.

The 4th-century BC mudbrick *temenos* wall of Coptos, under excavation in 1987.

although some Late Period and Middle Kingdom remains were also uncovered. The pottery corpus was predominantly of local manufacture, and there were surprisingly few imports or other closely datable artifacts among the finds. Nonetheless a sequence of four Hellenistic and four Roman assemblages was identified, ranging in date from the late 4th century BC to the 5th century AD.

Using the ceramic dates made possible by the stratified sequence from the Coptos excavation, the survey team has been able to distinguish chronologically distinct caravan routes through the Eastern Desert. The earlier, Hellenistic, tracks run south, not from Coptos but from the more southerly Nile port of Edfu to Berenice, a Ptolemaic foundation and the most southern port on the Red Sea. Later routes run more directly east from Coptos to the central and northern ports on the Red Sea established by the Romans, although the southern routes probably remained in use as well. The finds from the survey remain under study and will be published in the near future.

Opposite page: Distant view of a Roman caravan stop in the Eastern Desert on the route from Coptos to Quseir.

Below left: Modern inhabitants (as of 1991) of Qift's archaeological zone.

Below right: Hellenistic pottery from survey in the Eastern Desert.

Coptos and the Eastern Desert, Egypt

John Humphrey, University of Michigan

Nejib Ben Lazreg,
Institut National du Patrimoine

Hedi Slim, Institut National du Patrimoine

Lea Stirling, University of Manitoba

David Stone, University of Michigan

David Mattingly, University of Michigan
and University of Leicester

Directors

Photos courtesy of Leptiminus Archaeological Project

Leptiminus Archaeological Project, Tunisia
1990–1999

The site of Leptiminus in Tunisia and its surrounding hinterland have been the objects of an ongoing, long-term collaborative research project involving the University of Michigan, the University of Manitoba, and the Institut National du Patrimoine, Tunisia. The region witnessed a process of urban foundation, growth, decline, and abandonment across a time span of 1,200 years (ca. 500 BC–AD 700), a process leaving significant traces in the archaeological record. Since 1990 the Leptiminus Archaeological Project, a joint Tunisian-American-Canadian project, has conducted a regional survey of the area together with several excavations (since 1999, the project has been run under the auspices of the University of Manitoba).

An important port town that flourished under Roman rule, Leptiminus exported numerous agricultural products (including olive oil and *garum*, a popular fermented fish sauce), large-scale transport amphoras, and African Red Slip ware (a fine tableware much in demand throughout the Mediterranean from the 2nd through 7th centuries AD). These commodities from Leptiminus were traded throughout the Roman empire: from Italy, Spain, Portugal, and Britain in the West, to Egypt, Palestine, and Syria in the East. Both survey and excavation have also uncovered evidence of earlier Punic occupation as well as later Vandal, Byzantine, and Arab settlements.

Director and former Michigan student Lea Stirling (on the right) conversing near kilns.

The Excavations

The Leptiminus excavations produced an impressive variety of buildings with distinct functions, including cemeteries, houses, bathing establishments, a kiln complex, and a possible *fullonica* (a building used for washing and dyeing wool).

The cemeteries, which span the 2nd through 6th centuries AD and contained approximately 150 skeletons, are currently under study and will provide a valuable database for understanding the health, longevity, and burial practices of the settlement's ancient inhabitants.

A Roman bathhouse, covering an area of approximately 3,600 square meters, now ranks as one of the largest known in Roman North Africa. Excavations in 1992 revealed, under the floors of a heated room, courts and tunnels that were used by attendants to stoke the furnaces and fires. In the 6th century AD the bath complex was converted into an industrial area where large clay transport amphoras were produced. The archaeological remains also suggest that the building housed areas for metal and bone working, as well as butchery.

One excavated Roman house neatly traces the changing patterns of life in the eastern suburbs of the city. The building was transformed from a house with a fine mosaic of Venus in the *triclinium* (dining room), to an industrial area covered with ash, clay, and ceramic debris, to some kind of activity area that required the construction of a water channel, before finally, in the 5th and 6th centuries, being converted into a small cemetery.

Some of the most impressive finds from the Leptiminus excavations have come from a complex of seven Roman kilns. Although scholars have known for a long time that pottery

Below left: Three excavated tombs.

Below middle: Articulated skeleton in a cist grave.

Below right: Excavating a mosaic in one of the public baths.

made in North Africa was widely exported throughout the Roman empire, few African production sites have been closely studied. The Leptiminus kilns are among the first to be scientifically excavated and carefully published. Ranging in use from the 1st through the 3rd centuries AD, these kilns have yielded vast quantities of ceramics and misfired pots that will eventually shed light on patterns of both export markets and local consumption.

The Survey

Despite the rapid pace of development in the coastal region of Tunisia today, approximately 85% of the ancient town of Leptiminus remains under cultivation, and is thus ideally suited for archaeological survey. The town consists of approximately 1.5 square kilometers of gently rolling terrain planted with olive trees and bisected by two dry riverbeds (*wadis*). Remains of ancient structures, including more than 60 cisterns, an amphitheater, two baths, two aqueducts, and numerous walls, stand out among the olive trees. Preservation of

Pot sherds, separated by collection unit, drying in the sun.

Opposite page:

Top: Michigan students at work installing an exhibition of amphoras in the Lamta Museum.

Bottom: Exterior of the Lamta Museum with the entrance flanked by mosaics from local sites.

Below left: Excavation of a wall in the hinterland of Leptiminus.

Below right: Detail of an excavated mosaic in a Roman bath.

these remains, however, is poor owing to reuse of building materials in nearby medieval and modern settlements.

The Leptiminus survey focused on three primary goals. The first was to map and record each structure discovered in the course of fieldwalking. The second was systematically to examine the surface of the olive orchards for traces of past human activity, from pottery fragments, iron slag, and pieces of millstones, to building materials such as roof tiles, mosaic tesserae, and marble floor paving. The last was to "see beneath the soil" with the aid of devices that measure the earth's magnetism and resistance to electric currents, thus suggesting the probable locations of buried structures. Each of these goals has formed part of the archaeological survey of ancient Leptiminus and has helped build a field-by-field picture of the townscape.

Survey results identified an urban grid plan, located the probable town center (forum) of Leptiminus, and drew a picture of a city that does not conform to most standard views of Roman urbanism. The spatial distribution of artifacts clearly distinguishes an inhabited "public center" from a "productive periphery" on the town's outskirts. The latter area contains a high concentration of artifacts associated with ceramic production and with the smelting and smithing of imported ores. This evidence contrasts with one dominant perception of classical cities: that they were places of residence and of commerce (but not of production) and that they depended heavily on the countryside for any such production of goods. Leptiminus seems instead to have faced two ways: out to the sea toward the Mediterranean markets, and in toward a hinterland that included many landlocked towns. Other port towns like Leptiminus dotted the North African coast in antiquity and probably performed similar roles, participating in a range of urban craft activities for consumers who lay in both directions. Although Leptiminus provides archaeologists with a rare opportunity to study one of these ports, the

town itself was probably not particularly unique. Instead, it can stand as a representative of coastal settlements in the region that exported a range of manufactured goods and imported items for both agricultural tasks (iron ores and millstones) and luxury building (marble).

The Museum

A major component of the Leptiminus Archaeological Project involved the installation of a museum in the modern village of Lamta, on the site of the town's eastern baths. Completed in 1994, this museum now contains three galleries focusing on archaeological methods, discoveries at the site, and the Punic and Roman phases of Tunisia's history. The Tunisian Institute of Heritage took the lead in building the museum, while the Michigan team, headed by Jim Richerson and assisted by Dana Buck, a former exhibits preparator of the Kelsey Museum, designed the largest of the galleries. As one of four primarily educational museums in the country, it receives daily visits from groups of schoolchildren and tourists interested in Tunisia's classical history.

Leptiminus Archaeological Project, Tunisia

Jack Davis, University of Cincinnati

Susan E. Alcock, University of Michigan

John Bennet,
University of Wisconsin-Madison

Yannis Lolos, University of Ioannina

Cynthia Shelmerdine,
University of Texas-Austin

Eberhard Zangger, Geoarchaeological
Reconstructions, Zurich

Directors

Pylos Regional Archaeological Project, Greece
1991–1996

From 1991 to 1996 team members of the Pylos Regional Archaeological Project (PRAP) conducted an intensive archaeological surface survey in Messenia, in the southwestern part of the Greek Peloponnese. Observation and collection of surface finds, such as potsherds, roof tiles, and stone tools, allowed a reconstruction of the region's changing human occupation and utilization. The project's summer campaigns covered approximately 40 square kilometers (notionally centered around the Bronze Age administrative center known as the Palace of Nestor). Fieldwork doubled the number of sites previously known in this area and produced significant evidence for past human activity in the region, from its first occupation around 10,000 BC to the 19th century AD.

Thanks to surviving textual sources, scholars knew something of this region before the work of PRAP began. Linear B archives provided information about Bronze Age palatial life; the Greek historian Thucydides spoke of the "helots"—Messenians conquered and exploited by their neighbors, the Spartans, from the 8th to the early 4th century BC; the Roman traveler Pausanias recorded the region's myths, legends, and monuments in the 2nd century AD. Major archaeological excavations, especially projects at the Palace of Nestor and the well-fortified site of Messene—both popular tourist sites today—also contributed to our knowledge of the area.

Yet many questions remained unanswered. Where did the people live in the countryside?

View of the PRAP study area, with the Aigaleon mountain range in the background. Photo: J. F. Cherry.

Where did they cultivate their fields and how intensively? Where did they worship their gods in the countryside? How did all these patterns in the landscape alter through time, and with changing social and political circumstances?

PRAP can now offer answers to many of these questions. For example, it can be demonstrated where the people ruled by the Palace of Nestor (and who owed goods and services to it) dwelled and farmed, as well as the impact they had on the surrounding natural environment. A different pattern of settlement and of cult practice has been traced for the period of Spartan control, giving some unique insights into how helots survived their centuries of oppression. Significant changes—more cities, more villages, more farms, more shrines—appear in the years following Messenian liberation in 370 BC. The Roman period witnessed a growing interest in coastal settlement, as people increasingly looked west to the Italian peninsula. PRAP team members discovered, for example, a large coastal villa site, complete with a bath, mosaics, and fishpond—all mapped by the PRAP survey team.

It should be emphasized that PRAP was a multidisciplinary project, involving not only archaeologists but also anthropologists, historians, archivists, geologists, hydrologists, and botanists. Throughout the course of the project, many sources of evidence were used to supplement what was discovered in the field. The presence of a "port" for the Palace of Nestor has been argued through geological and hydrological studies. Pollen analysis has demonstrated a noteworthy increase in olive cultivation, apparently coinciding with the archaeologically documented increase in settlement following the region's liberation from Sparta. Finally, archival work on tax records in Istanbul and Venice has been coordinated with archaeological evidence to illuminate Messenia's history under Ottoman and Venetian rule.

A PRAP team member explores the remains of the hypocaust (underfloor heating system) of a Roman bath; the piles of round hypocaust tiles (to left) are very characteristic of such structures. This bath was discovered as part of a large coastal villa complex. Photo: S. E. Alcock.

A PRAP survey team in action. Photo: S. E. Alcock.

Opposite page:

Top left: Roof tile fragments from a survey site, showing the bags and tags used in the field. Photo: S. E. Alcock.

Top right: Pottery illustration aided rapid analysis of survey finds. Photo: S. E. Alcock.

Bottom left: Artifact collection in the field. Photo: S. E. Alcock.

Bottom right: A burial, with long bones visible, found at a PRAP site. The grave was exposed through bulldozing. Photo: S. E. Alcock.

Donald Keller, The American Center of Oriental Research

Malcolm Wallace, University of Toronto

Directors, 1989–

Photos courtesy of Donald Keller

Southern Euboea Exploration Project, Greece
Michigan involvement: 1996, 2000, 2002, 2005

The Southern Euboea Exploration Project (SEEP) is a multidisciplinary research project in the region of ancient Karystia on Euboea, the second largest island of Greece. Well known from classical texts, the political region of Karystia controlled a vital link in the system of maritime trade routes and was home to an international sanctuary to Poseidon. Until the 1980s, however, the area was *terra incognita* archaeologically: only three places had been tested by excavation, and surveys had catalogued fewer than ten sites. Moreover, the archaeological record for the prehistoric occupation of southern Euboea was a virtual blank.

In order to document the archaeological remains from this understudied region in Greece, SEEP conducted a three-year (1984–87) intensive survey of the Paximadhi peninsula,

Town of Karystos with Mount Ochi looming in the background.

a largely barren 22-square-kilometer area west of the bay of Karystos. Further work was carried out in the territory east of the bay in 1989, 1990, and 1993. The survey has now located and recorded more than 300 sites (concentrations or scatters of finds) dating from the later part of the Neolithic to Turkish times (ca. 4000 BC–AD 1820), traced several premodern routes in the rugged interior around the eastern bay, and conducted two salvage excavations of classical sites.

Michigan's efforts concentrated on the approximately 20 prehistoric findspots spanning the end of the Neolithic to the middle of the Early Bronze Age (ca. 4000–2500 BC). Although the sample of prehistoric sites is small, distinct settlement patterns can be detected. Ridge tops and southern slopes, near springs, appear to have been the preferred locations for settlement during the Final Neolithic, while the Early Helladic inhabitants selected coastal settings. The single Middle Helladic site is set inland on a prominent hilltop. To the extent that sherd and lithic scatters can determine size, it would appear that the prehistoric sites are generally quite small. Close ceramic parallels, particularly with the island of Keos, and the abundance of obsidian from the island of Melos suggest that southern Euboea was part of a larger network of communication and exchange that included at least the Cyclades and Attica. No longer seen as an economic backwater in prehistoric times, southern Euboea must now be viewed as supporting a number of small, early sites that had close contact with contemporary settlements in the Cyclades and the mainland.

Unfortunately, recent modern development has gradually obliterated much of the region's archaeological remains. Large tracts of land, formerly reserved for farming and grazing, are now being rezoned for hotels and summer houses, and the construction of a new sewer plant has buried at least one known prehistoric site under several meters of sand.

Below left: Typical sherds from the Final Neolithic site of Plakari (ca. 4000–3000 BC).

Below right: The Early Bronze Age site of Aghios Georgios (excavated by a team of Greek archaeologists), today covered by an electrical plant.

Opposite page: Examining abandoned columns in an ancient Roman quarry north of Karystos.

New roads cut into Cape Mnima for the construction of summer houses. The new buildings will eventually cover most of the known archaeological sites in the area.

The Paximadhi peninsula and the town of Karystos viewed from the site of an ancient Roman quarry. (Note the partially buried marble column in the foreground.)

Southern Euboea Exploration Project, Greece

Janet Richards, University of Michigan
Director

The Abydos Middle Cemetery Project, Egypt
1995–

The large and multicomponent site of Abydos (ancient *3bdw*) lies about 400 kilometers south of Cairo in upper Egypt, on the west bank of the Nile River. Located at the margin of desert and floodplain, Abydos was never a capital or seat of central government during the Dynastic era (3100–332 BC) but was always an important ceremonial site for both royal and private individuals. The site was ultimately identified as the burial place of the god Osiris, king of the underworld, and the primary entrance to that next world. As such, it was maintained as a coherent conceptual landscape for more than 3,000 years.

The primary burial ground for nonroyal individuals in the Old Kingdom was a part of the site called the "Middle Cemetery" by modern excavators. Previously investigated in the 1860s by the flamboyant first director of the Egyptian Antiquities Organization, Auguste Mariette, the Middle Cemetery was known to have yielded inscriptions from the graves of important Sixth Dynasty officials (2407–2260 BC). Among these inscriptions discovered in the early years of Egyptian archaeology was the long and colorful autobiography of Weni the Elder. This life story, a well-known piece of ancient Egyptian literature, was most likely excavated from the monumental surface chapel of a tomb, called a mastaba (Arabic for "bench," describing the shape of these structures). A later series of British missions in the late 19th and early 20th centuries provided evidence that a substantial lower-order cemetery of far simpler graves bracketed the area from which these inscriptions came; however, because of the haphazard nature of Mariette's work, the development and significance of the elite component of the provincial cemetery, which he described as located on a "high

Abydos crew in 2001, with Janet Richards, director (second from right, front).

hill," had never been well understood. No subsequent excavators worked in Mariette's portion of the Middle Cemetery until the Kelsey Museum applied for permission to resume excavations there in 1995.

The University of Michigan received permission from the Supreme Council of Antiquities (Ministry of Culture, Egypt) to investigate the entire Middle Cemetery at Abydos and began to work in this cemetery in cooperation with the Pennsylvania-Yale-Institute of Fine Arts/New York University Expedition, which was then excavating the ancient town in which Mariette's officials would have lived. Two initial seasons of topographic mapping and surface survey of ceramic, architectural, and artifactual remains resulted in the creation of a detailed contour map of the entire Middle Cemetery and confirmation that late Old Kingdom ceramic material and mudbrick construction did indeed dominate this area. Two full-scale seasons of excavation (1999 and 2001) and two further seasons of magnetic survey (2002 and 2004) later, the spatial organization of the cemetery began to emerge, along with new

General view of the site of Abydos and cliffs beyond.

Opposite page: View into burned burial chamber of Weni the Elder. Photo: Y. Kobylecky and R. Fletcher.

facts regarding the late Old Kingdom individual Weni the Elder, and the political agenda underlying the development of the Old Kingdom mortuary landscape at Abydos.

The University of Michigan work has demonstrated that use of the Middle Cemetery at Abydos had a definite starting point in the later Old Kingdom, most likely motivated by a political desire to promote the central government in the provinces. For several hundred years after the founding of the Early Dynastic royal cemetery near the cliffs, in about 3100 BC, no private burial was allowed anywhere else on the low desert plateau in North Abydos. The Michigan excavations have documented that this taboo was kept in place until sometime in the Fifth Dynasty, about 700 years later, when at least four monumental elite tombs for late Old Kingdom officials were built on the highest prominence of the plateau, flanked by an extensive pattern of tidy rows of subsidiary mastaba graves. Reflecting an idealized view of social relations, the graves of lower-order individuals were placed on an isolated ridge to the northeast, separated by space and topography from the occupants of the elite graves.

In 1999 the Michigan team excavated a broad expanse in the central part of the Middle Cemetery, exposing two large Old Kingdom elite tomb complexes, two subsidiary mastabas and their associated shafts, and a level of votive activity focused on these Old Kingdom structures but dating to the Middle Kingdom 500 years later. One of these tombs proved to be that of Weni the Elder, the governor of Upper Egypt. The tomb's superstructure consisted of a massive square structure nearly 30 meters long on each side and more than 15 meters tall. The team rediscovered the chapel from which Weni's famous biography originally came, as well as new inscriptions and statuary relating to his career; team members also excavated a series of graves situated around his monument, including both buri-

Work in the Project's sherd yard.

The Abydos Middle Cemetery Project, Egypt

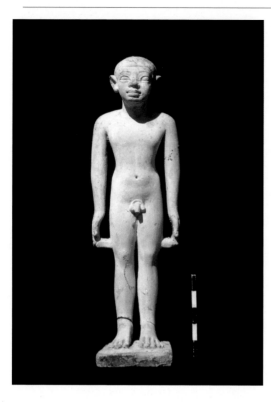

Above: Limestone statuette of Weni as a boy excavated from his tomb. Photo: K. D. Turner.

At right: Reconstruction: the architectural components of Weni's grave. G. Compton.

als contemporary with his own and a small Saïte Period cemetery (ca. 685–525 BC) located around the top of his burial shaft.

In 2001 work focused on excavating the burial shafts and chambers for Weni's tomb and that of an overseer of priests, Nekhty, as well as expanding the horizontal exposure of the cemetery surface. The excavation of the chambers yielded unforeseen evidence about the fate of these tombs during the political disturbances of the First Intermediate Period: Weni's chamber was thoroughly burned, perhaps as a deliberate strike against the province by the central government; and it emerged that Nekhty's burial chamber had been usurped from an Old Kingdom official named Idi, possibly as part of the same upheaval.

Elsewhere excavations in 2001 revealed a continuation of the pattern of rows of subsidiary mastabas radiating from these two elite monuments; and results from the two seasons of magnetic survey documented an extraordinarily vast landscape of numerous rows of such graves, as well as the existence of at least two further elite complexes. One of these is most likely that of Weni's father, the Vizier Iuu, documented by Lepsius in the 19th century but subsequently "lost."

The Kelsey Museum plans to continue the long-term investigation of the archaeological remains and their relation to ancient Egyptian society and history in the Middle Cemetery at Abydos in the future. Goals for the project include a close examination not only of the monumental inscribed tombs of the elite but also of the non-elite graves sharing one of the largest provincial cemetery landscapes of the later third millennium BC.

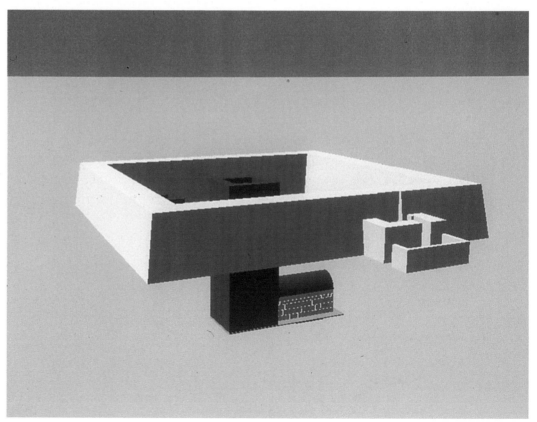

View to the destroyed offering chapel of Weni the Elder. Photo: J. Parsons.

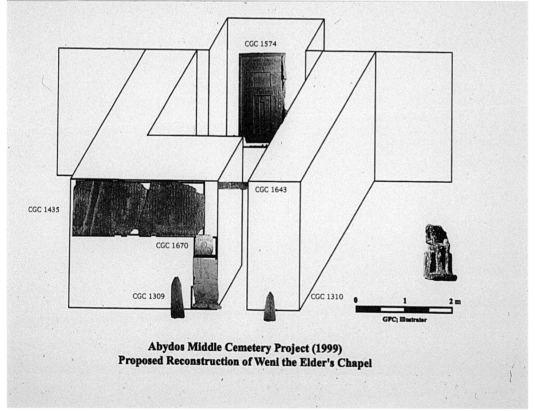

CGC 1574

CGC 1435

CGC 1643

CGC 1670

CGC 1309

CGC 1310

0   1   2 m

GFC₁ Illustrator

Abydos Middle Cemetery Project (1999)
Proposed Reconstruction of Weni the Elder's Chapel

Reconstruction showing probable original location of Weni's biographical slab and other objects in his offering chapel. G. Compton and A. Wilburn.

Sharon C. Herbert, University of Michigan

Andrea M. Berlin, University of Minnesota

Directors

Photos courtesy of Sharon C. Herbert

Kedesh of the Upper Galilee, Israel

1997–

This Kelsey field project follows up and expands on questions raised by earlier Museum excavations at Sepphoris and Tel Anafa. Tel Kedesh is the largest unexcavated tel site in Upper Galilee, occupying an area of ca. 9 to 10 hectares. It is located on the land of Kibbutz Malkia, some 450 meters above sea level and about 10 kilometers northwest of Hazor. Situated in one of the richest agricultural zones of modern Israel, the area of Kedesh and the Upper Galilee has been home since antiquity to a tapestry of cultural and ethnic groups, from the Israelite tribe of Naphthali to Phoenicians from the nearby city of Tyre. Many successive layers of occupation can be seen in the road cut along the

Aerial photo of Tel Kedesh, looking northeast.

north edge of the tel, and a Roman temple, preserved to architrave height, stands to the east of the mound.

The site is mentioned in the Old Testament, most importantly as one of the "cities of refuge" for those guilty of unintentional homicide. It also appears in several of the histories from the period of Graeco-Roman occupation. We learn from Zenon, a 3rd-century BC traveler from Egypt, that Kedesh was a flourishing farming village in his time, providing him with food supplies and the luxury of a bath. From First Maccabees we hear that Kedesh was the Greek campsite for a battle between Jonathan and the Seleucid king Demetrias in 145 BC and that its pagan occupants fled after the Jewish victory. According to Josephus, Kedesh was again a Tyrian outpost and stronghold in the first centuries BC and AD; and it served as an encampment for the Roman general Titus at the beginning of the First Jewish Revolt.

The University of Michigan/University of Minnesota expedition received a permit in 1997 from the Israel Antiquities Authority to conduct excavations at Kedesh. Since then, work has focused on the remains of the Hellenistic and Roman periods, with particular interest in identifying the site's population(s) and their interactions with the Phoenicians, Jews, Greeks, and Romans living throughout this area. The ancient texts indicate that Kedesh passed in and out of Tyrian control from the Persian period onward and came, at least briefly, under the rule of the Hasmoneans and, later, perhaps that of Herod the Great. The social and economic effects of such shifts between Jewish and Phoenician control are special objects of study.

Tel Kedesh and its environs are demonstrably rich in remains from the Early Bronze Age to modern times and have clear potential to elucidate the issues outlined above as well as many other questions. A site of this size demands extensive pre-excavation exploration and testing to insure, insofar as possible, that major field seasons will yield maximum information

Michigan students excavating a 2nd-century BC house, 1997.

At right: Stamped clay seal impressions with images of deities; impressions range in size from ca. 1 to ca. 1.5 centimeters.

Below: Laying the lines in preparation for the magnetometry survey, 1998.

Kedesh of the Upper Galilee, Israel

86

with minimal destruction. To these ends two short exploratory seasons in 1997 and 1998 aimed to determine the location and extent of the Hellenistic and Roman remains and to prepare the site for excavation. Preliminary activities included a locational survey, two small probe trenches, a magnetometry survey on the southern tel, and contour mapping of the entire site. Results of the 1997 and 1998 work demonstrated the presence of significant and accessible Hellenistic remains on the southern tel, some portion of which most likely belonged to the Tyrians who abandoned the site after the defeat of Demetrias by the Maccabees in 145 BC.

Major field seasons were undertaken in the summers of 1999 and 2000. The work concentrated at the southern end of the lower mound, where magnetometry showed the potential for a large structure. Excavations there uncovered approximately 20% of an enormous Hellenistic building (56 meters east-west by 40 meters north-south), abandoned shortly after the middle of the 2nd century BC and built over a Persian-period predecessor. The size, internal fittings, and especially the finds of the Hellenistic building—including an archive represented by 2,043 stamped clay seal impressions—indicate that this was a public administrative center, probably housing either the governor of the eparchy of Galilee or the *strategos* of Coele-Syria. The finds show compelling affinities with the material culture of Hellenistic Phoenicia with a considerable admixture of Greek elements. Some parts of the building were reoccupied shortly after its abandonment by people living in a much less grandiose manner, but whose material culture also reflects Hellenistic Phoenician influences. These findings can inform larger historical issues, including the Persian administration of the region from the 5th century BC and relations among the Tyrians, the Seleucids, and the Jews in the first half of the 2nd century BC. The nature and timing of the abrupt dissolution of this administrative base just after the middle of the 2nd century BC reflect significant changes in the balance of power in the region.

Below left: Mapping the Roman temple in relation to Tel Kedesh.

Below right: Phoenician semi-fine pottery found on a Hellenistic floor.

Susan E. Alcock, University of Michigan and Brown University

John F. Cherry, University of Michigan and Brown University

Armen Tonikyan,
Union of Architects, Yerevan

Mkrtich Zardaryan, Institute of Archaeology and Ethnography, National Academy of Sciences, Yerevan

Directors

Photos courtesy of John F. Cherry

The Vorotan Project, Armenia
2005–

The Vorotan Project, an international, collaborative archaeological project based in Armenia, formally began fieldwork in August 2005, following preliminary reconnaissance trips in 2004. The Project focuses on the country's southernmost province, Syunik, sandwiched between Iran, Azerbaijan, and the Azeri enclave polity of Naxçivan. Running through this region is the Vorotan River, long a major conduit of trade and intercommunication in the southern Caucasus—a region that itself lies at a significant crossroads, controlling the corridor between the Black and the Caspian Seas, between Russia to the north and western Asia to the south. The project's goal is to carry out multiyear fieldwork in this sensitively located, but little-known, area beginning in a self-contained river basin around the village of Angeghakot.

Much sound archaeological work has been undertaken in Armenia, especially in the decades when it formed part of the USSR. Over the years, numerous excavations have been conducted at sites of the Bronze Age and the Urartian period (ca. 800–600 BC), as well as at some of classical and medieval date; for the latter eras, the results of excavations at places such as Armavir, Artashat, Dvin, Garni, and Tsakahovit are best known. Most attention, however, has been paid to the Ararat Plain (in the vicinity of the modern capital city of Yerevan) and areas to its north and east (for example, near Lake Sevan). By contrast, very little systematic work has been done in Syunik in the deep south, although occasional finds (e.g., a tomb with rich grave goods indicating a strong Mediterranean influence) and the existence of a remarkable standing-stone complex known as the "Armenian Stonehenge" (Karahunj/Zorats Karer) have always made clear that this is potentially rich archaeological territory.

Apart from a desire to begin more systematic exploration of an unknown, but clearly key, zone in the southern Caucasus, the Vorotan Project has two other principal objectives.

Below left: A view across the Vorotan River to the steep-sided, Yervandid-period site of Balak, on whose summit test excavations took place in 2005.

Below right: Part of the prehistoric complex of standing-stone alignments, burial, and settlement at Karahunj/Zorats Karer (Syunik marz, southern Armenia).

First, it experiments with methodologies that have hitherto not often been deployed in this part of the world, not least archaeological survey (i.e., the intensive, systematic reconnaissance of regional landscapes for traces of past human activity). This type of work, aimed at the reconstruction of changing human landscapes over time (revealing, for example, trends in settlement patterns or sacred geography), has been attempted once before, and briefly, in the southern Caucasus, but its suitability to this region requires further assessment.

Second, although regional work is inherently diachronic in nature, the project is according special attention to the later first millennium BC and early first millennium AD. These important centuries—known, after local dynasties, as the Yervandid, Artaxiad, and Arsacid periods, and roughly equivalent to the Achaemenid, Classical, Hellenistic, Roman, and Parthian periods in the chronologies of cultures to the west and south—have mostly been studied "from the top down": that is, through the partial excavation of capital cities (sites such as Armavir or Artashat). Patterns in economic and social life below that elite level, and beyond the Ararat Plain, remain an enigma. The pottery chronologies essential for studying sites of this period are as yet poorly understood; to refine their understanding, the project in 2005 undertook some limited excavation sondages on two very promising sites (Shaghat I, Balak), already identified as having occupation of this date. The final component of the Project's first season was the beginnings of a systematic mapping and study of the mortuary landscape of the study region. The area is dotted with an extraordinary palimpsest of stone-built tombs of various types, which require careful analysis to unravel patterns in their use and reuse over time.

The Vorotan Project joins a growing number of American and European projects now working in the Black Sea region and in the Caucasus, projects that are building communicative bridges to the strong tradition of Soviet archaeology. Archaeology in these areas had previously tended to be marginalized in Western eyes, being neither fully "Mediterranean" nor "Near Eastern." In this way, the Project continues the Kelsey Museum's rich heritage of working on the edges of the classical world, as well as broadening the scope and ambitions of classical archaeology.

A robbed Bronze Age cist tomb with capstone covering in the necropolis of Uits.

Below left: Intensive survey tract-walking, with a little interference from cows.

Below right: A carved Christian *khachkar* (memorial stone) at a late medieval village.

Bibliography

Antioch of Pisidia, Turkey

Harrer, G. A.

1925   The Latin inscription from Antioch. *American Journal of Archaeology* 29: 429–33.

Mitchell, S., and M. Waelkens (eds.)

1998   *Pisidian Antioch: The Site and Its Monuments*. London: Duckworth with the Classical Press of Wales.

Robinson, D. M.

1924a   A preliminary report on the excavations at Pisidian Antioch and at Sizma. *American Journal of Archaeology* 28: 435–44.

1924b   A new Latin economic edict from Pisidian Antioch. *Transactions of the American Philological Association* 55: 5–20, 248.

1926a   *The Deeds of Augustus as Recorded on the Monumentum Antiochenum*. Baltimore: Johns Hopkins Press.

1926b   The Res Gestae Divi Augusti as recorded on the Monumentum Antiochenum. *American Journal of Philology* 47: 1–54.

1927   The discovery of a prehistoric site at Sizma. *American Journal of Archaeology* 30: 26–50.

Karanis, Egypt

Boak, A. E. R. (ed.)

1933   *Karanis: The Temples, Coin Hoards, Botanical and Zoölogical Reports. Seasons 1924–31*. University of Michigan Studies: Humanistic Series 30. Ann Arbor: University of Michigan Press.

Boak, A. E. R., and E. E. Peterson

1931   *Karanis: Topographical and Architectural Report of Excavations during the Seasons 1924–28*. University of Michigan Studies: Humanistic Series 25. Ann Arbor: University of Michigan Press.

Gazda, E. K.

1978   *Guardians of the Nile: Sculptures from Karanis in the Fayoum (c. 250 BC–AD 450)*. Ann Arbor: Kelsey Museum of Archaeology, University of Michigan.

Gazda, E. K. (ed.), with a new preface and updated bibliography by T. G. Wilfong

2004   *Karanis, an Egyptian Town in Roman Times: Discoveries of the University of Michigan Expedition to Egypt (1924–1935)*. Kelsey Museum Publication 1. Kelsey Museum of Archaeology, University of Michigan.

Haatvedt, R. A., and E. E. Peterson; E. M. Husselman (ed.)

1964   *Coins from Karanis: The University of Michigan Excavations 1924–1935*. Ann Arbor: Kelsey Museum of Archaeology.

Harden, D. B.

1936   *Roman Glass from Karanis Found by the University of Michigan Archaeological Expedition in Egypt, 1924–29*. University of Michigan Studies: Humanistic Series 41. Ann Arbor: University of Michigan Press.

Husselman, E. M.

1952   The granaries of Karanis. *Transactions of the American Philological Association* 83: 56–73.

1953   The dovecotes of Karanis. *Transactions of the American Philological Association* 84: 81–91.

1979   *Karanis Excavations of the University of Michigan in Egypt, 1928–1935: Topography and Architecture. A Summary of the Reports of the Director, Enoch E. Peterson*. University of Michigan Kelsey Museum of Archaeology Studies 5. Ann Arbor: University of Michigan Press.

Johnson, B.

1981   *Pottery from Karanis: Excavations of the University of Michigan*. University of Michigan Kelsey Museum of Archaeology Studies 7. Ann Arbor: University of Michigan Press.

Kelsey, F. W.

1927   Fouilles américaines à Kom Ousim (Fayoum). *Chronique d'Égypte* 5: 78–79.

Minnen, P. van

1994   House-to-house enquiries: an interdisciplinary approach to Roman Karanis. *Zeitschrift für Papyrologie und Epigraphik* 100: 227–51.

1995   Deserted villages: two Late Antique town sites in Egypt. *Bulletin of the American Society of Papyrologists* 32: 41–56.

Pollard, N.

1998   The chronology and economic condition of late Roman Karanis: an archaeological reassessment. *Journal of the American Research Center in Egypt* 35: 147–62.

Shier, L. A.

1978   *Terracotta Lamps from Karanis, Egypt: Excavations of the University of Michigan*. University of Michigan Kelsey Museum of Archaeology Studies 3. Ann Arbor: University of Michigan Press.

Thomas, T. K.

2001   *Textiles from Karanis, Egypt, in the Kelsey Museum of Archaeology: Artifacts of Everyday Life*. Ann Arbor: Kelsey Museum of Archaeology, University of Michigan.

Wilfong, T. G.

1995   Karanis Objects. In N. Thomas (ed.), *The American Discovery of Ancient Egypt*, 223–30. Los Angeles: Los Angeles County Art Museum.

Wilson, L. M.

1933   *Ancient Textiles from Egypt in the University of Michigan Collection*. University of Michigan Studies: Humanistic Series 31. Ann Arbor: University of Michigan Press.

Carthage, Tunisia

Bruehl, E.

1997–   To the Lady Tanit, Face of Baʻal, and to Our Lord Baʻal Hammon: Kelsey squeezes
2000   from the 1925 excavation in the sanctuary of Tanit at Carthage. *The University of Michigan Museums of Art and Archaeology Bulletin* 12: 42–69.

Dunbabin, K.

1985   Mosaics of the Byzantine period in Carthage: problems and directions of research. *Carthage VII. Actes du Congrès* 2. *Cahiers des études anciennes* 17: 9–30.

Ellis, S.

1985   Carthage in the seventh century: an expanding population? *Carthage VII. Actes du Congrès* 2. *Cahiers des études anciennes* 17: 31–42.

Ennabli, A. (ed.)

1992   *Pour sauver Carthage: exploration et conservation de la cité punique, romaine et byzantine.* Paris: UNESCO; Tunis: Institut national d'archéologie et d'art.

Ennabli, L.

1987   Results of the International Save Carthage Campaign: the Christian monuments. *World Archaeology* 18: 291–311.

Garrison, M. B.

1990   A late Roman/early Byzantine cemetery at Carthage: the University of Michigan excavations at Carthage. *Archaeological News* 15: 23–29.

Harden, D. B.

1927   Punic urns from the precinct of Tanit at Carthage. *American Journal of Archaeology* 31: 297–310.

Humphrey, J. H.

1978   North African news letter 1. *American Journal of Archaeology* 82: 511–20.

1985   Le Musée Paléochrétien de Dermech. *Carthage VII. Actes du Congrès* 2. *Cahiers des études anciennes* 17: 127–39.

Humphrey, J. H. (ed.)

1976   *Excavations at Carthage 1975 Conducted by the University of Michigan* 1. Kelsey Museum Fieldwork Series. Tunis: Cérès Productions.

1977   *Excavations at Carthage 1976 Conducted by the University of Michigan* 3. Kelsey Museum Fieldwork Series. Ann Arbor: Kelsey Museum, University of Michigan.

1978a   *Excavations at Carthage 1975 Conducted by the University of Michigan* 2. Kelsey Museum Fieldwork Series. Ann Arbor: Kelsey Museum, University of Michigan.

1978b   *Excavations at Carthage 1976 Conducted by the University of Michigan* 4. Kelsey Museum Fieldwork Series. Ann Arbor: Kelsey Museum, University of Michigan.

1980   *Excavations at Carthage 1977 Conducted by the University of Michigan* 5. Kelsey Museum Fieldwork Series. New Delhi: Thomsons Press.

1981   *Excavations at Carthage 1977 Conducted by the University of Michigan* 6. Kelsey Museum Fieldwork Series. Ann Arbor: Kelsey Museum, University of Michigan.

1982   *Excavations at Carthage 1977 Conducted by the University of Michigan* 7. Kelsey Museum Fieldwork Series. Ann Arbor: Kelsey Museum, University of Michigan.

1988   *The Circus and a Byzantine Cemetery at Carthage* I. Ann Arbor: University of Michigan Press.

Humphrey, J. H., and J. G. Pedley

1978   Roman Carthage. *Scientific American* 238.1: 110–20.

Kelsey, F. W.

1926   *Excavations at Carthage 1925: A Preliminary Report*. New York; London: MacMillan.

Norman, N. J.

1986   The American excavations in the Roman circus at Carthage. *Carthage VIII. Actes du Congrès* 3. *Cahiers des études anciennes* 18: 81–100.

Pedley, J. G. (ed.)

1980   *New Light on Ancient Carthage*. Ann Arbor: University of Michigan Press.

Richerson, J., and S. Stevens

1994   From monastery to museum in Carthage. *Museum News* 73.4: 24–27, 65.

Stevens, S. T.

1993   *Bir el Knissia at Carthage: A Rediscovered Cemetery Church* 1. *Journal of Roman Archaeology* Supplementary Series 7. Kelsey Museum Fieldwork Series. Ann Arbor: Kelsey Museum, University of Michigan; Tunis: Institut national du patrimoine.

1995   A late-Roman urban population in a cemetery of Vandalic date at Carthage. *Journal of Roman Archaeology* 8: 263–70.

Stevens, S. T., and J. Richerson

1994   Between Caesar and Mohammed: uncovering Christian Carthage. *Minerva* 5.1: 33.

Wells, C. M.

1982   Recent excavations at Carthage: a review article. *American Journal of Archaeology* 86: 293–96.

Seleucia-on-the-Tigris, Iraq

Debevoise, N. C.

1934   *Parthian Pottery from Seleucia on the Tigris*. University of Michigan Studies: Humanistic Series 32. Ann Arbor: University of Michigan Press.

1938   When Greek and Oriental cultures met at Seleucia. *Asia* 38: 746–51.

1941   The origin of decorative stucco. *American Journal of Archaeology* 45: 45–61.

Hopkins, C.

1937   Michigan excavations at Seleucia-on-the-Tigris, 1936–1937. *Michigan Alumnus Quarterly Review* 10: 28–32.

1939   A bird's-eye view of Opis and Seleucia. *Antiquity* 13: 440–48.

Hopkins, C. (ed.)

1972   *Topography and Architecture of Seleucia-on-the-Tigris*. Ann Arbor: University of Michigan.

Ingen, W. van

1939   *Figurines from Seleucia on the Tigris, Discovered by the Expeditions Conducted by the University of Michigan with the Cooperation of the Toledo Museum of Art and the Cleveland Museum of Art 1927–1932*. University of Michigan Studies: Humanistic Series 45. Ann Arbor: University of Michigan Press.

McDowell, R. H.

1933   The excavations at Seleucia on the Tigris. *Papers of the Michigan Academy of Science, Arts and Letters* 18: 101–19.

1935a *Coins from Seleucia on the Tigris.* University of Michigan Studies: Humanistic Series 37. Ann Arbor: University of Michigan Press.

1935b *Stamped and Inscribed Objects from Seleucia on the Tigris.* University of Michigan Studies: Humanistic Series 36. Ann Arbor: University of Michigan Press.

Savage, E.

1976 *Seleucia-on-the-Tigris: An Exhibition of the Excavations at Seleucia, Iraq, by the University of Michigan, 1927–32, 1936–37.* Ann Arbor: Kelsey Museum of Archaeology, University of Michigan.

Waterman, L.

1931 *Preliminary Report upon the Excavations at Tel Umar, Iraq, Conducted by the University of Michigan and the Toledo Museum of Art.* University of Michigan Publications. Ann Arbor: University of Michigan Press.

1933 *Second Preliminary Report upon the Excavations at Tel Umar, Iraq, Conducted by the University of Michigan, the Toledo Museum of Art, and the Cleveland Museum of Art.* University of Michigan Publications. Ann Arbor: University of Michigan Press.

Sepphoris, Israel

Gazda, E. K., and E. A. Friedland (eds.)

1997 *Leroy Waterman and the University of Michigan Excavations at Sepphoris, 1931: "The Scientific Test of the Spade."* Ann Arbor: Kelsey Museum of Archaeology, University of Michigan.

Meyers, E. M., E. Netzer, and C. L. Meyers

1992 *Sepphoris.* Winona Lake, IN: Eisenbrauns.

Nagy, R. M., C. L. Meyers, E. M. Meyers, and Z. Weiss (eds.)

1996 *Sepphoris in Galilee: Crosscurrents of Culture.* Winona Lake, IN: Eisenbrauns.

Netzer, E., and Z. Weiss.

1994 *Zippori.* Jerusalem: Israel Exploration Society.

Waterman, L.

1937 *Preliminary Report of the University of Michigan Excavations at Sepphoris, Palestine, in 1931.* Ann Arbor: University of Michigan Press.

Soknopaiou Nesos (Dimé), Egypt

Boak, A. E. R.

1932 Dimê. *American Journal of Archaeology* 36: 522–23.

Boak, A. E. R. (ed.)

1935 *Soknopaiou Nesos: The University of Michigan Excavations at Dimê in 1931–32.* University of Michigan Studies: Humanistic Series 39. Ann Arbor: University of Michigan Press.

Root, M. C.

1984 *The Art of Seals: Aesthetic and Social Dynamics of the Impressed Image from Antiquity to the Present.* Ann Arbor: Kelsey Museum of Archaeology, University of Michigan.

Terenouthis, Egypt

Grunow, M. D.

1995   Amulets from Tomb 4, Kom Abou Billou, Egypt. In J. E. Richards and T. G. Wilfong, *Preserving Eternity: Modern Goals, Ancient Intentions. Egyptian Funerary Artifacts in the Kelsey Museum of Archaeology*, 45–46. Ann Arbor: Kelsey Museum of Archaeology, University of Michigan.

Haeckl, A. E., and K. C. Spelman (eds.)

1977   *The Gods of Egypt in the Graeco-Roman Period.* Ann Arbor: Kelsey Museum of Archaeology, University of Michigan.

Hooper, F. A.

1961   *Funerary Stelae from Kom Abou Billou.* The University of Michigan Kelsey Museum of Archaeology Studies 1. Ann Arbor: Kelsey Museum of Archaeology.

McCleary, R. V.

1987   *Portals to Eternity: The Necropolis at Terenouthis in Lower Egypt. The University of Michigan's Reconnaissance Expedition to Kom Abou Billou, the Necropolis of Ancient Terenouthis (March to April 1935).* Ann Arbor: Kelsey Museum of Archaeology, University of Michigan.

Monastery of St. Catherine at Mount Sinai, Egypt

Forsyth, G. H.

1964   Island of faith in the Sinai wilderness. *National Geographic* 125: 82–108.

1968   The Monastery of St. Catherine at Mount Sinai: the church and fortress of Justinian. *Dumbarton Oaks Papers* 22: 1–19.

Forsyth, G. H., and K. Weitzmann

1973   *The Monastery of Saint Catherine at Mount Sinai: The Church and Fortress of Justinian* 1. *Plates.* Ann Arbor: University of Michigan Press.

Forsyth, G. H., and K. Weitzmann, with J. Galey (ed.)

1980   *Sinai and the Monastery of St. Catherine.* Givatayim, Israel: Massada Publishing.

Weitzmann, K.

1964   Mount Sinai's Holy Treasures. *National Geographic* 125: 109–27.

1973   *Illustrated Manuscripts at St. Catherine's Monastery on Mount Sinai.* Collegeville, MN: St. John's University Press.

1976   *The Monastery of Saint Catherine at Mount Sinai: The Icons* 1. *From the Sixth to the Tenth Century.* Princeton, NJ: Princeton University Press.

1982   *Studies in the Arts at Sinai: Essays.* Princeton, NJ: Princeton University Press.

Weitzmann, K., M. Chatzidakis, K. Miatev, and S. Radojčić

1965   *Frühe Ikonen. Sinai, Griechenland, Bulgarien, Jugoslawien.* Vienna; Munich: Anton Schroll.

Weitzmann, K., and G. Galavaris

1990   *The Monastery of Saint Catherine at Mount Sinai: The Illuminated Greek Manuscripts* 1. Princeton, NJ: Princeton University Press.

Qasr al-Hayr al-Sharqi, Syria

Grabar, O.

1970a   Le nom ancien de Qasr al-Hayr al-Šarqī. *Revue des études islamiques* 38.2: 251–66.

1970b   Preliminary report on the third season of excavations at Qasr al-Hayr Sharqi. *Annales archéologiques arabes syriennes* 20: 1–10.

1970c   Three seasons of excavations at Qasr al-Hayr Sharqi. *Ars Orientalis* 8: 65–85.

Grabar, O., R. Holod, J. Knustad, and W. Trousdale

1978   *City in the Desert: Qasr al-Hayr East.* Harvard Middle Eastern Monographs 23–24. Cambridge, MA: Distributed for the Center for Middle Eastern Studies of Harvard University by Harvard University Press.

Holod-Tretiak, R.

1970   Qasr al-Hayr al-Sharqi; a mediaeval town in Syria. *Archaeology* 23: 221–32.

Apollonia, Libya

Goodchild, R. G.

1971   *Kyrene und Apollonia.* Zurich: Raggi Verlag.

Goodchild, R. G., J. G. Pedley, and D. White

1976   *Apollonia, the Port of Cyrene: Excavations by the University of Michigan 1965–1967.* Supplements to *Libya Antiqua* 4. Tripoli: Department of Antiquities.

McAleer, J. P.

1980   *A Catalogue of Sculpture from Apollonia.* Supplements to *Libya Antiqua* 6. Tripoli: Department of Antiquities.

Pedley, J. G.

1967   Excavations at Apollonia, Cyrenaica: second preliminary report. *American Journal of Archaeology* 71: 141–47.

White, D.

1966   Excavations at Apollonia, Cyrenaica: preliminary report. *American Journal of Archaeology* 70: 259–65.

Cyrene, Libya

Buttrey, T. V., and I. McPhee

1997   *The Extramural Sanctuary of Demeter and Persephone at Cyrene, Libya: Final Reports* 6. *1. The Coins. 2. Attic Pottery.* D. White, series ed. University Museum Monograph 97. Philadelphia: University Museum, University of Pennsylvania.

Kocybala, A.

1999   *The Extramural Sanctuary of Demeter and Persephone at Cyrene, Libya: Final Reports* 7. *The Corinthian Pottery.* D. White, series ed. University Museum Monograph 95. Philadelphia: University Museum, University of Pennsylvania, for the Libyan Department of Antiquities.

Lowenstam, S., M. B. Moore, P. M. Kenrick, and T. Fuller

1987   *The Extramural Sanctuary of Demeter and Persephone at Cyrene, Libya: Final Reports 3. 1. Scarabs, Inscribed Gems, and Engraved Finger Rings. 2. Attic Black Figure and Black Glazed Pottery. 3. Hellenistic and Roman Fine Wares. 4. Conservation of Objects.* D. White, series ed. University Museum Monograph 66. Philadelphia: University Museum, University of Pennsylvania, for the Libyan Department of Antiquities.

Schaus, G. P.

1985   *The Extramural Sanctuary of Demeter and Persephone at Cyrene, Libya: Final Reports 2. The East Greek, Island, and Laconian Pottery.* D. White, series ed. University Museum Monograph 56. Philadelphia: University Museum, University of Pennsylvania, for the Libyan Department of Antiquities.

Warden, P. G., A. Oliver, P. J. Crabtree, and J. Monge

1990   *The Extramural Sanctuary of Demeter and Persephone at Cyrene, Libya: Final Reports 4. 1. The Small Finds. 2. Glass. 3. Faunal and Human Skeletal Remains.* D. White, series ed. University Museum Monograph 67. Philadelphia: University Museum, University of Pennsylvania, for the Libyan Department of Antiquities.

White, D.

1973   Two girls from Cyrene: recent discoveries from the Sanctuary of Demeter and Persephone. *Opuscula Romana* 9: 207–15.

1975   Archaic Cyrene and the cult of Demeter and Persephone. *Expedition* 17.4: 2–15.

1984   *The Extramural Sanctuary of Demeter and Persephone at Cyrene, Libya: Final Reports 1. Background and Introduction to the Excavations.* University Museum Monograph 52. Philadelphia: University Museum, University of Pennsylvania, in association with the Libyan Department of Antiquities.

1993   *The Extramural Sanctuary of Demeter and Persephone at Cyrene, Libya: Final Reports 5. The Site's Architecture, Its First Six Hundred Years of Development.* University Museum Monograph 76. Philadelphia: University Museum, University of Pennsylvania, for the Libyan Department of Antiquities.

White, D., I. F. Bald, L. Schenk, S. Tutweiler, B. R. MacDonald, G. Schaus, M. Bloom, and K. Chance

1976   Seven recently discovered sculptures from Cyrene, Eastern Libya. *Expedition* 18.2: 14–32.

Tel Anafa, Israel

Berlin, A. M.

1993   Italian cooking vessels and cuisine from Tel Anafa. *Israel Exploration Journal* 43: 35–44.

1997   From monarchy to markets: the Phoenicians in Hellenistic Palestine. *Bulletin of the American Schools of Oriental Research* 306: 75–88.

1999   What's for dinner? The answer is in the pot. *Biblical Archaeology Review* 25.6: 46–55, 62.

Berlin, A., and K. W. Slane

1997   *Tel Anafa* 2.1. *The Hellenistic and Roman Pottery: the Plain Wares; the Fine Wares.* *Journal of Roman Archaeology* Supplementary Series 10.2.1. Kelsey Museum Fieldwork Series. Ann Arbor: Kelsey Museum of Archaeology.

Herbert, S. C.

1973   Tel Anafa, 1973. *Israel Exploration Journal* 23: 113–17.

1978   Tel Anafa, 1978. *Israel Exploration Journal* 28: 271–74.

1979a   Tel Anafa 1978: preliminary report. *Bulletin of the American Schools of Oriental Research* 234: 68–83.

1979b   Tel Anafa 1979. *Muse* 13: 16–21.

1980   Tel Anafa 1980. *Muse* 14: 24–30.

1981   Tel Anafa, 1979, 1980. *Israel Exploration Journal* 31: 105–7.

1982   Tel Anafa, 1981. *Israel Exploration Journal* 32: 59–61.

1984   Tell Anafa (1981). *Revue biblique* 91: 235–39.

1987   Tel Anafa, 1986. *Israel Exploration Journal* 37: 272–73.

1993   The Greco-Phoenician settlement at Tel Anafa: a case study in the limits of Hellenization. In A. Biran, J. Aviram, and A. Paris-Shadur (eds.), *Biblical Archaeology Today, 1990. Proceedings of the Second International Congress on Biblical Archaeology, Jerusalem, June–July 1990*, 118–25. Jerusalem: Israel Exploration Society.

1994   *Tel Anafa* 1. *Final Report on Ten Years of Excavation at a Hellenistic and Roman Settlement in Northern Israel. Journal of Roman Archaeology* Supplementary Series 10.1. Kelsey Museum Fieldwork Series. Ann Arbor: Kelsey Museum of Archaeology.

Dibsi Faraj, Syria

Harper, R. P.

1974a   Excavations at Dibsi Faraj, Northern Syria, 1972. *Les annales archéologiques arabes syriennes: revue d'archéologie et d'histoire* 24: 25–29.

1974b   Second preliminary report on excavations at Dibsi Faraj. *Les annales archéologiques arabes syriennes: revue d'archéologie et d'histoire* 24: 31–37.

1975   Excavations at Dibsi Faraj, Northern Syria, 1972–1974: a preliminary note on the site and its monuments. *Dumbarton Oaks Papers* 29: 319–38.

1980   Athis—Neocaesareia—Qasrin—Dibsi Faraj. In J.-Cl. Margueron (ed.), *Le moyen Euphrate, zone de contacts et d'échanges*: *Actes du Colloque de Strasbourg 10–12 mars 1977*, 327–48. Strasbourg: Université des sciences humaines de Strasbourg.

Wilkinson, T. J.

1976   Soil and sediment structures as an aid to archaeological interpretation: sediments at Dibsi Faraj, Syria. In D. A. Davidson and M. L. Shackley (eds.), *Geoarchaeology: Earth Science and the Past*, 277–87. London: Duckworth.

Paestum-Poseidonia, Italy

Greco, E.

1999   *Paestum: Past & Present*. Rome: Vision.

Greco, E., and F. Longo

2000   *Paestum: scavi, studi, ricerche. Bilancio di un decennio: 1988–1998*. Tekmeria 1. Paestum (Salerno): Pandemos: Fondazione Paestum.

Johannowsky, W., J. G. Pedley, and M. Torelli

1983   Excavations at Paestum 1982. *American Journal of Archaeology* 87: 293–303.

Miller Ammerman, R.

1991   The naked standing goddess: a group of archaic terracotta figurines from Paestum. *American Journal of Archaeology* 95: 203–30.

2002   *The Sanctuary of Santa Venera at Paestum* 2. *The Votive Terracottas*. Ann Arbor: University of Michigan Press.

Pedley, J. G.

1985   Excavations at Paestum 1984. *American Journal of Archaeology* 89: 53–60.

1990   *Paestum: Greeks and Romans in Southern Italy*. London: Thames and Hudson.

Pedley, J. G., and M. Torelli

1984   Excavations at Paestum 1983. *American Journal of Archaeology* 88: 367–76.

1993   *The Sanctuary of Santa Venera at Paestum. Il Santuario di Santa Venera a Paestum*. Archaeologia perusina 11. Rome: Giorgio Bretschneider.

Coptos and the Eastern Desert, Egypt

Herbert, S. C.

1999   Quft/Qift (Coptos). In K. A. Bard (ed.), *Encyclopedia of the Archaeology of Ancient Egypt*, 656–57. London; New York: Routledge.

Herbert, S. C., and A. Berlin

2002   Coptos: architecture and assemblages in the Sacred Temenos from Nectanebo to Justinian. In *Autour de Coptos. Actes du colloque organisé au Musée des Beaux-Arts de Lyon (17–18 mars 2000). Topoi: Orient-Occident* Supplément 3, 73–115. Lyon: Maison de l'Orient méditerranéen.

2003   *Excavations at Coptos (Qift) in Upper Egypt, 1987–1992. Journal of Roman Archaeology* Supplementary Series 53. Kelsey Museum Fieldwork Series. Portsmouth, RI: Journal of Roman Archaeology.

Leptiminus Archaeological Project, Tunisia

Ben Lazreg, N.

2002   Roman and Early Christian burial-complex at Leptiminus: first notice. *Journal of Roman Archaeology* 15: 336–45.

Ben Lazreg, N., and D. J. Mattingly

1992   *Leptiminus (Lamta): a Roman Port City in Tunisia* 1. *Journal of Roman Archaeology* Supplementary Series 4. Ann Arbor: University of Michigan.

Stirling, L. M., D. J. Mattingly, and N. Ben Lazreg

2001   *Leptiminus (Lamta)* 2. *The East Baths, Cemeteries, Kilns, Venus Mosaic, Site Museum, and Other Studies. Journal of Roman Archaeology* Supplementary Series 41. Kelsey Museum Fieldwork Series. Portsmouth, RI: Journal of Roman Archaeology.

Stirling, L. M., D. L. Stone, N. Ben Lazreg, A. Burke, K. Carr, R. J. Cook, J. Dore, A. Giambrone, S. Jezik, S. Johnston, B. Longfellow, B. Meiklejohn, C. Meiklejohn, J. Moore, A. Opait, H. Park, I. Schrüfer-Kolb, B. L. Scherriff, and D. Welle
2000   Roman kilns and rural settlement: interim report of the 1999 season of the Leptiminus Archaeological Project. *Echos du monde classique/Classical Views* 40.19: 170–224.

Stone, D. L., L. M. Stirling, and N. Ben Lazreg
1998   Suburban land-use and ceramic production around Leptiminus (Tunisia): Interim report. *Journal of Roman Archaeology* 11: 304–17.

Pylos Regional Archaeological Project, Greece

Alcock, S. E., A. Berlin, A. B. Harrison, S. Heath, N. Spencer, and D. L. Stone
2005   Pylos Regional Archaeological Project VII: historical Messenia, Geometric through late Roman. *Hesperia* 74: 147–209.

Davis, J. L. (ed.)
1998   *Sandy Pylos: An Archaeological History from Nestor to Navarino.* Austin: University of Texas Press.

Davis, J. L., S. E. Alcock, J. Bennet, Y. Lolos, and C. Shelmerdine
1997   The Pylos Regional Archaeological Project I: overview and the archaeological survey. *Hesperia* 66: 391–494.

Davis, J. L., F. Zarinebaf and J. Bennet
2000   The Pylos Regional Archaeological Project III: Sir William Gell's itinerary in the Pylia and regional landscapes in the Morea in the Second Ottoman Period. *Hesperia* 69: 343–80.

Davies, S.
2004   Pylos Regional Archaeological Project VI: administration and settlement in Venetian Navarino A.D. 1700. *Hesperia* 73: 59–120.

Fleischman, J.
1997   The archaeologists who wouldn't dig: uncovering one of the most storied sites in antiquity—without touching a shovel. *The Sciences* 37.3: 12–14.

Lee, W. E.
2001   The Pylos Regional Archaeological Project IV: change and a human landscape in a modern Greek village in Messenia. *Hesperia* 70: 49–98.

Stocker, S. R.
2003   Pylos Regional Archaeological Project V: Deriziotis Aloni: a small Bronze Age site in Messenia. *Hesperia* 72: 341–404.

Zangger, E., M. E. Timpson, S. B. Yazvenko, F. Kuhnke, and J. Knauss
1997   The Pylos Regional Archaeological Project II: landscape evolution and site preservation. *Hesperia* 66: 548–641.

Southern Euboea Exploration Project, Greece

Keller, D. R.
1982   Final Neolithic pottery from Plakari, Karystos. In P. Spitaels (ed.), *Studies in South Attica* 1, 47–67. Miscellanea Graeca 5. Ghent: Comité des fouilles Belges en Grèce.

Keller, D. R., and M. B. Wallace

1986   The Canadian Karystia Project. *Echos du monde classique/Classical Views* 30.5: 155–59.

1987   The Canadian Karystia Project, 1986. *Echos du monde classique/Classical Views* 31.6: 225–27.

1988   The Canadian Karystia Project: two classical farmsteads. *Echos du monde classique/Classical Views* 32.7: 151–57.

1990   Pre-modern land routes in Southern Euboia. *Echos du monde classique/Classical Views* 34.9: 195–99.

Kosso, C.

1996   A late Roman complex at Palaiochora near Karystos in Southern Euboia, Greece. *Echos du monde classique/Classical Views* 40.15: 201–30.

Talalay, L. E., T. Cullen, D. R. Keller, and E. Karimali

2005   Prehistoric occupation in Southern Euboea: an overview. In N. M. Kennell and J. E. Tomlinson (eds.), *Ancient Greece at the Turn of the Millennium: Recent Work and Future Perspectives*, 21–44. Athens, Greece: Canadian Archaeological Institute at Athens.

The Abydos Middle Cemetery Project, Egypt

Herbich, T., and J. Richards

2005   The loss and rediscovery of the Vizier Iuu at Abydos: magnetic survey in the Middle Cemetery. In E. Czerny (ed.), *Festschrift Manfred Bietak*, 141–49. Vienna: Denkschriften der Gesamtakademie.

Richards, J.

1999   Conceptual landscapes in the Egyptian Nile valley. In W. Ashmore and A. B. Knapp (eds.), *Archaeologies of Landscape: Contemporary Perspectives*, 83–100. Malden, MA: Blackwell Publishers.

2001a   Quest for Weni the Elder. *Archaeology* 54.3: 48–49.

2001b   Text and context in late Old Kingdom Egypt: the archaeology and historiography of Weni the Elder. *Journal of the American Research Center in Egypt* 39: 75–102.

2002   Time and memory in ancient Egyptian cemeteries. *Expedition: Magazine of the University of Pennsylvania Museum* 44.3: 16–24.

2003   The Abydos cemeteries in the late Old Kingdom. In Z. Hawass (ed.), *Egyptology at the Dawn of the Twenty-first Century: Proceedings of the Eighth International Congress of Egyptologists, Cairo* 1, 400–407. Cairo and New York: American University in Cairo Press.

2005   *Society and Death in Ancient Egypt: Mortuary Landscapes of the Middle Kingdom.* Cambridge: Cambridge University Press.

Kedesh of the Upper Galilee, Israel

Ariel, D. T., and J. Naveh

2003   Selected inscribed sealings from Kedesh in the Upper Galilee. *Bulletin of the American Schools of Oriental Research* 329: 61–80.

Berlin, A. M., T. Ball, R. Thompson, and S. C. Herbert

2003   Ptolemaic agriculture, "Syrian Wheat," and *Triticum aestivum. Journal of Archaeological Science* 30: 115–21.

Herbert, S. C.

2003   Excavating ethnic strata: the search for Hellenistic Phoenicians in the Upper Galilee of Israel. In S. Kane (ed.), *The Politics of Archaeology and Identity in a Global Context*, 101–13. Boston: Archaeological Institute of America.

2004–5 The Hellenistic archives from Tel Kedesh (Israel) and Seleucia-on-the-Tigris (Iraq). *The University of Michigan Museums of Art and Archaeology Bulletin* 15: 65–86.

Herbert, S. C., and A. M. Berlin

2000   Excavations at Kedesh 1997–99. *Israel Exploration Journal* 50: 118–23.

2003   A new administrative center in Persian and Hellenistic Galilee: preliminary report of the University of Michigan/University of Minnesota excavations at Kedesh. *Bulletin of the American Schools of Oriental Research* 329: 13–59.

The Vorotan Project, Armenia

Kiesling, B., and R. Kojian

2005   *Rediscovering Armenia: An Archaeological/Touristic Gazetteer and Map Set for the Historical Monuments of Armenia*, 2nd edition. Yerevan: Graphic Design Studio.

Smith, A. T., and K. Rubinson (eds.)

2004   *Archaeology in the Borderlands: Investigations in Caucasia and Beyond.* Cotsen Institute of Archaeology at UCLA, Monograph 47. Los Angeles: Cotsen Institute of Archaeology.

Xnkikyan, O. S.

2002   *Syunik during the Bronze and Iron Ages.* Barrington, RI: Mayreni Publishing.

Photo Credits

Images for the following sites are housed in various photo archives of the Kelsey Museum:

- Antioch of Pisidia, Turkey
- Karanis, Egypt
- Carthage, Tunisia (images on pages 20, 21, and 22)
- Seleucia-on-the-Tigris, Iraq
- Sepphoris, Israel
- Soknopaiou Nesos (Dimé), Egypt
- Terenouthis, Egypt
- Qasr al-Hayr al-Sharqi, Syria
- Apollonia, Libya
- Cyrene, Libya

Other photo credits:

- Carthage, Tunisia: Jennifer P. Moore, Trent University (images on page 23); Naomi Norman, University of Georgia (images on pages 24 and 25)
- Monastery of St. Catherine at Mount Sinai, Egypt: Michigan-Princeton-Alexandria Expedition to Mount Sinai
- Tel Anafa, Israel: Sharon C. Herbert, University of Michigan
- Dibsi Faraj, Syria: Dumbarton Oaks, Trustees for Harvard University, used by permission
- Paestum-Poseidonia, Italy: James Higginbotham, Bowdoin College (images on pages 55 and upper and middle right images on page 57); John G. Pedley, University of Michigan (images on page 54 and 56 and upper and lower left and lower right images on page 57)
- Coptos and the Eastern Desert, Egypt: Sharon C. Herbert, University of Michigan
- Leptiminus Archaeological Project, Tunisia: Lea Stirling, University of Manitoba; David Stone, Florida State University
- Pylos Regional Archaeological Project, Greece: Susan Alcock, Brown University; John Cherry, Brown University
- Southern Euboea Exploration Project, Greece: Donald Keller, American Center of Oriental Research
- The Abydos Middle Cemetery Project, Egypt: Janet Richards, University of Michigan
- Kedesh of the Upper Galilee, Israel: Sharon C. Herbert, University of Michigan
- The Vorotan Project, Armenia: Susan Alcock, Brown University; John Cherry, Brown University